Sorrow Bread

Sorrow Bread

Poems 1984–2015

Selected and New

Mark Cox

Serving House Books

Sorrow Bread: Poems 1984–2015

ISBN: 978-0-9977797-3-8

Cover art: *Intellectual Property*, by MJ Cunningham
www.mj-art.com

Serving House Books logo by Barry Lereng Wilmont

Published by Serving House Books
Copenhagen, Denmark and Florham Park, NJ
www.servinghousebooks.com

Member of The Independent Book Publishers Association

Friends of Poets & Writers

First Serving House Books Edition 2017

For My Parents,

Wayne B. Cox II
and
June K. Cox

with love and gratitude

Contents

8. After Rain

In the Petrified Forest,

rain
still
falls

1. Inner Rooms

Pail of Eggs

The land is only ground now.
No footpaths, no ruins, not even
a slab where the root cellar stood.
Still, there is the slap of a screen door
when my son exits the car,
the squeal of a well pump
when my youngest wants juice,
and there I am in the sprouting field corn,
back brown as mud, crew cut blond
as the hens' eggs I've never put down.

The adults are still patient,
awaiting breakfast in their graves,
the bacon still diminishing
in the blackened pan.
No one knows where I am.
Half-grown, tousled candle of a boy,
I have walked to where the vulture landed,
to his runway of symmetrical rows
where the fox, lame with poison,
swallowed her last breath.
Face up. Eyes widened and clear.
Wherever I go from here,
I will not go hungry.

The Word

I get in between the covers as quietly as I can.
Her hand is on my pillow and I put my face as close
as I can without waking her up. We made salad yesterday
and her fingertips still smell of green pepper and onions.
I feel homey, almost safe, breathing this, remembering
the way we washed the vegetables under cold water, peeled,
then sliced them with the harmless little knife her sister
gave us for Christmas. I feel childish and gently pull
the blanket over my head, barely touching my lips
to the short, ragged fingernails she chews while talking to
her mother on the phone. These days there's so much bad news
from home. Old people who keep living and living awfully,
babies who stop breathing for no reason at all.
I am so close to her that if I were to speak one word
silently, she would feel it and toss the covers to one side,
and for this reason I'll say nothing as long as I can.
Let the sheet stiffen above us, I have nothing to say.
Not about their lives or my own life.
Not about the branches so weighted with snow
they don't brush our window anymore.
Not about the fact that the only way I can touch anymore
at all, the only way I can speak, is by trying not to.
"What's left, what's left, what's left," my dog breathes
in his sleep. Lately, I snore badly in a language
only he understands. I've been trying so hard to teach,
I've been trying so hard to switch bodies
with the young people in my classes,
that last week, when he woke me and wanted to go out,
I took his face in my hands and told him not to be afraid.
"You know so much already," I said.
"You are talented and young, you have something to give people,
I wouldn't lie to you."
Rita told this story as we sat around the salad with friends,

noting, as she did, how the dog closed his eyes and basked.
Sleep is also the only place I can type with more than three
fingers, I said. But I thought, it's true, all this,
I speak best and most fully in my sleep. When my heart
is not wrapped in layer after layer of daylight, not prepared
like some fighter's taped fist.
She sleeps, her hand next to my mouth, the number
for the ATM fading on its palm.
The word starts briefly from between my lips, then turns back.
The word sifts deeper into what my life is.

Carrier

Those tires I heard as I turned ten
        our car windows cracked
                parents and siblings fast asleep

those trucks which forsook our rest stop
        compelled across midnight into Tennessee
                a resonant mist-soaked unremitting hum

                have traveled 28,412,000 miles now
all of it in me

The Door

There's no discernible point of origin,
and this is exactly what wakes you—
the thin whistle,
diluted by time,
a former lover within you,
boiling water for tea
in an efficiency banished so deeply into mind,
it might as well be another side of the world.
This is what it means to see clearly
the clock/radio's cold, green digits
as a room number that keeps changing,
a suite of coordinates
reserved for your death,
and though you don't know where,
tonight an insect rubs its legs there,
or a man purses his lips and spits out
the last of his wanting toward a nurse,
or perhaps it's as simple as a distant phone,
but you know the sound
and refuse it an answer.
It's just three o'clock in the morning,
just the wind, just tires on the road,
just the dry hinges of a door
you passed by quickly,
thinking it was closed.

All That Shimmers and Settles Along the Roads
of Our Passage

After seventeen years, I return home to my ex-wife,
without the cigarettes and bread,
without the woman and children I left her for,
older, empty-handed, and yet
to the same clothes
still in the same drawers,
as if nothing has changed.

My torn t-shirt is still splotched with paint
across her left breast,
her hair has not gone gray at the temples,
and she does not ask a single question:
not *where have you been,*
not *how could you,*
not *where were you when I needed you,*

just, *hey baby* and a smile,
the Vermont air cold,
the old mattress flat on the floor,

because the frame and box springs are still in the Ryder truck,
because my first students have not entered the classroom,
I have yet to fall in love with my own bourbon-soaked voice,
our dog has not died arthritic and stroke-plagued,

there is, instead, the kitchen faucet still running,
the beans rinsed and splayed in the colander,
and there isn't the slightest anger in her voice,
that I have missed a good dinner,
that I will have to warm it up if I want any,
it's ok, in fact, if I let the dog out
one last time and *just come on to bed.*

And so I could re-enter
the dream's cold, pine-paneled walls,
knots bleeding through their sealer,
I could, after seventeen years, step back
into that unblemished body,
shrug back on the aspirations and worries,
and begin again, sorrow by sorrow,
to destroy her love for me,
my own confidence and faith.
Because this is the nature of time,
or at least the relation of our nature to time,
to idealize that kitchen,
the string beans on the counter,
the dog bed by the door—
if we can still see it, it must be real,
it must still exist there,
not frozen in stasis,
but still playing itself out,
forever, without repeating,
as the moment it is.

It is my dream, then, that is the repetition,
my return, the problem,
but if I don't extend my hand into it,
do not turn loose the knob,
if I can step back outside, quickly, before we touch,
press my face to the storm door,
it is clear the young man I was
and the young woman she was
can still love each other
and have not turned away.

Pompeii

The laborers, lying down at night,
Their tents layered with silt,
settled into the postures
they exhumed daily,
must have thought:

one moment we're on our way to work,
the next we're work for someone else;
one moment we're making love, the next
we've become what someone else loves to do,
brought to light by the caress of chisel and hammer,
the lascivious ogling of lab techs and scholars.

But you can only guess, just as this promontory
can only look out over all that dissolves it,
the sunlight a glaze along the horizon of its going,
seabirds risen, then settling
like cinders on the water.

And so the grist of time turns out to be
not ashes, not bone shards, not even lint,
but the bread crumbs of a last meal
mostly eaten, then brushed free
to the earth.

You have tried to stay still,
God knows, you have tried
to stay pressed to the table edge,
your legs like the legs of tables,
your arms like the arms of chairs,
but here it is at last,
that destination you have been approaching
since you were a speck.

The knife on its side,
the spoon and fork arched on their backs,
the napkin crumpled, a hand
reaching over your shoulder to clear
the place setting, snuff the candle.

What is best loved betrays most acutely.
The athlete's body, the scholar's mind,
the made thing gone numb and clenched,
refusing shape.

Like beached trawlers after the storm of God,
hulls split seam to seam,
flung up and gleaming,
here are your childhood selves
contorted in their beds,
face up in their pasts,
that compressed soil caving
into half-open mouths,
the slender fingers of dream
plucking at their tendons.

So your sun rises, as the workers rose again
to squat over simple stoves,
to simmer and stir and sip and swallow,
in the clear dawn cold of each day
all history comes down to.

Treasure

Axe heads and sledges, musket balls and elixir bottles,
the earth cleans its room without having to be told;
as if putting tools back neatly into the case of the ground,
history knows precisely where each of us goes.

This is close to what the boy must think, he who already
has a boy buried inside him, who, like a nine-volt battery,
can be removed and handled. His head is a bottle cap,
his torso a wound mass of baling wire. And when the boy
holds this small self he can sit ringed with mushrooms
on the decaying stump of his father's childhood
and feel every turn the earth makes
driving home through the dark.

He has excavated an entire vacation.
He has passed this wand over acres of pull-tabs
and coffee cans teeming with grubs and beetles.
But this is his first unearthing of unadulterated sorrow,
of all he cannot remember, or forget, or undo.

He is only ten. The metal detector, which now rests
chirping across his knees, is destined for his dim closet.
But it has found him and that was worth everything.
And now that he has found himself,
these glances of light, the uncouplings
of birdsong, of leaf from leaves,
what if he were to step forward into that future,
his heart thudding like a thermos in a lunch pail,
what if he were to rise like mist from the forest floor
then turn from the flint-nicked trowel of the season?

He sees it is like those grainy silent comedies
in which someone is asked to volunteer,

then the entire cast but one steps back.
Someone has to do it. Someone has to be the past
with its drawn, saddened, weary face,
someone has to be the bullet-pocked backdrop,
that retaining wall of shame and wailing,
the collector of evidence
against which all else is measured.

Morality Play

General Lee has suffered visibly
since his divorce, gone genuinely gray
yet less able to stay in character—
propped on his horse by Prozac
and behavioral therapy.
The dimpled tin flask?

It may or may not
be part of the act.
But the bulge in his tunic,
the burial mound between
his heart and epaulet,

that's a Nokia phone.
He can feel it vibrate
even as he draws his saber to charge—
his daughter again, impatient,
worried about the science fair project
or that Miguel boy or both.

In our fathers' mansions are many rooms,
each staircase lit by a proper woman's dress,
exploding outward from the waist,
bright as muzzle flash. In this fashion,
the must-tinged, curated odors
of death and disrepair

are dispelled by antebellum grace,
a gay waltz superimposed
on the gallows and scorched earth
of unconditional surrender.
And here, in the white cavalry tents
of dressing rooms and canteens,

might be found the re-embodied cast,
their corpses stacked four deep,
breaking for coffee and short bread
flecked with the ash of last night's fires,
warming themselves, palms first
at the steam of Starbuck's cups,

as if at barrels of tallow or pitch,
the rendered fats of human appetite,
our ongoing morality play
of canned spectacle and irrevocable orders,
eternal figures of will and submission,
spit-shines gilding our bloody past.

Push forward on the left flank,
mount and survey what's won.
Rear up on the grand white stallion,
hurrah the troops with hat in hand,
pause for photo ops. Done.
Rivulets of audience empty grassy lots

and now, what is the strategy
for his newly sexual daughter's suitor
and the papier-mâché volcano
she needs to erupt by Monday.

Donald

When chimpanzees are threatened, they band together at first
and touch their hands to each other's mouths
as if to say, "Yes, I'm here."

Something like the way a man might find himself
hurrying down the hall, running
a callused thumb over his kid's lips, saying,
" I know you're afraid," again, again, and again,
even after the child has leaned back into the limbs of sleep.

The chimps will then venture out, away from the group—
on land in the savannah,
across the tree, in the trees—
throwing what they can at the enemy in an underhand motion
or breaking off sticks and approaching it.

Today at work, in the washroom mirror,
while trying to get the water in my cupped hands to my face
without spilling any,
I saw little smears of paint everywhere
and realized how often I'd touched my own face during the day:
a decision in front of the candy machine; rubbing my eyes,
the bridge of my nose. Though I didn't know,

it rained all morning and into afternoon while I painted
the superstructure of the ceiling of that factory, by which
means now, strapped in and idling next to the 7-11,
my hand inside a small paper bag,
listening to the new silence of a new exhaust system,
the almost-evening spring light seems clean here
on the parking lot. From outside,

through the glass of the windshield

16

and then the glass of the storefront,
half-clearly and half-convoluted
by the reflection of both bars across the street,
I can see a kid in a tuxedo, his hands two bulges
in the pockets of his pants, smiling at the counterman.

If I didn't know him, he could be just any young guy
holding his head in such a way it's obvious
his shirt neck's too tight;
but I do, and I know
the graft marks on the side of his face that isn't towards me
and I know the thick, kind speech that betrays brain damage.

His date is in there too, fussing now and again
with his chopped hair—a pretty woman, tall, fluid, sure
when she parked and got out a minute ago—and I've found
what I was feeling in the bag for, and I'm in reverse now,
backing up from the window, trying to enjoy one of those smiles
one smiles remembering something,

when they appear wholly, carrying nothing,
while the counterman neglects a customer to watch them do so,
and as the boy walks along the sidewalk, across the entryway
he's swept and shoveled out a thousand times,
he turns the leathery, birth-scarred left side of his face,
and turning her attention once more to the hair above its ear,
she touches him briefly there.

I'm turning the wheel with the flat palm of one hand,
scratching (which is a sign of indecision in chimps)
my chest with the cold root beer in my other,
and hesitating at the exit, thinking I could so easily
get sad now, because I know it's his sister,
but when I look in the rear-view mirror, look back, I can see
that his friend who works nights has come out to wave,

and think instead of how always the chimps return to touch

and be touched again, that if you were here, you'd know
what I was about to say, and as if you were here, I feel, bringing
the cool rim of that can to my lips, your fingers and pull away.

Inner Rooms

To contain so much hatred when the hated are dead,
where does one put it? It fills hanged purses
in closets, the suit pockets, cigar tins,
it gleams on cuff links and tie clasps
in their crushed velvet spring-boxes.

If you cannot find it, it may be you
suspended in the blown glass perfume stopper,
beside the shoehorns and mortuary rulers,
the free pencils that will never be sharpened,
in the paper clips, twisted, confused, shackled
one to another.

Where, having been given the satin folds of lingerie,
their sheen and shadow like an ocean in a drawer,
do you begin?
Your parents' room become museum.
The hat boxes heaped with photos,
sorted by decade, most unlabeled,

is this where it is? An answer? The essence?
Beside the revolver under his handkerchiefs,
in your bronzed baby shoes, laced forever,
in the see-through model
of the human circulatory system,
in those branching blues and reds,

or in the broken Westclox, its alarm set for 1944?
The loose pearl she salvaged, but never restrung?
The gouged surface of the Vaseline?
Where is that spark that made the world inevitable,
where is that apron, that blew in furls
around your mother's waist

as she stood on the front steps to call you in?

This is as deep as it goes. There is no more to them
than you. Your skin thinned,
your inner lives grown cold. There is no key
taped to a drawer bottom, not one fingerprint
on one dusty light bulb, no trace of the moment
before they let go, turned their faces to the wall.

Is this what love is, this rage
to have and know? To string the pearls,
to wear that moon on a strand of her long hair,
orbiting the heart, translucent testicle,
tiny lump in the breast?
What was it that was done? Who did it

and said the others needn't know?
Or who did not smile and kiss you here and here,
who did not set the cocktail down to smooth your hair
with two cool hands.

How can you know,
when nothing can ever open the wall safe of silence?
And you must fashion the world again
without the painting that hung over it,
without certainty, without closure,
without them.

Alcohol

In this faded family photo—
Horton, Kansas, '36—
they are just two farmhands in overalls,
kept, by a bowed velvet cordon,
from some gala event. Except it's a rattlesnake
strung between them,
five, perhaps, six feet in length
and thick as my young father's outstretched arms.
One might think his pride, that is,
anticipation of us,
would dictate looking at the camera,
but he seems to be eyeing
the slick, intricate patterns of risk
now relaxed in his hand.
Then again, given his uneasy, strained half-smile,
he could be checking my grandfather's grip,
the snake so freshly dead,
making sure any reflex is under control—
suspecting the undulant weight of it,
that he could never really let go.

The Pale and Hairless Ankles of the Sun

On Wednesdays I can't breathe right.
As if my tongue were a clenching fist.
Whatever I'd like you to hear me say then
is too much larger than I am.
Wednesdays—I can't bear them.
They're like coffins surfacing
from deep in my blood.
They're like logs so immense
you can't get your arms around them;
I can't carry them inside.
And Thursdays! Today, not one kind word
and the newspaper was so heavy
it disappeared into the ground.
It caused my legs to fall asleep.
Wednesdays want so much to be saved
that each one pulls more sky in after it.
Each Thursday has more earth in its mouth.

Outtakes

Dusk's embroidery, vivid, vast,
richly sutured
with infinite accident.

Autumn has come, its woods stark,
only our own passing
sweeps leaves back into the trees.

Film upon film, decade into decade,
so many figures absorbed,
and still the screen is never filled.

Clotheslines, pale, bowed
pulley to pulley, span
the rest home courtyard,
blistered with rain.

Like skiers, drops of rain drawn
diagonally down the window.
Some survive longer than others.

We are alone.
It only seems that the moon
is a flashlight pointed at you.

That barefoot boy at Woolworths
still steers his coin-operated car
through 1961 without a coin.

Eventually, a woman
hands you a jar to open
and you can't.

2. Sorrow Bread

The Tunnel at the End of the Light

The summer my body began to fit,
living seemed as fluid
as putting my arm through a sleeve—
when I threw crusts of bread in the air,
they became birds,
when I held her,
I held myself—
nothing, nothing resisted,
and since it was my job to turn on
the pool lights—
a single lever controlled all six—
evening was over when I said so,
and sometimes as I restocked
the clip rack with chips,
she would stop balancing the ketchup bottles
atop each other,
and as they drained,
she would touch me, tenderly,
in the small of my back
along the rim of tan line,
as if applying pressure
to a wound no one else knew about,
and some nights,
before letting our footprints evaporate,
before driving away
to our separate neighborhoods,
we had the pool to ourselves—
our city below, it awakened and slept
one light at a time, but the pool
was one brilliant, unified blue
and we would press against
the warm lenses of the lights,
as if they were the portholes

of some vast ship sealed so tight
as to have survived sea-bottom,
fearing the worst, knowing
that it sometimes takes minutes
for small cuts to bleed,
and that in two or three months
when this light had poured out of us,
there would be shadows in our veins
too big for one body.

Lemon Icing

(after Auden)

About suffering they were never wrong.
How it takes place while dad smears on
The BBQ sauce, while mother adjusts
A cafe-style umbrella. Here, the boy rests
His cheek on the rim of a diving pool, squints
At the glazed trail of his sister's footprints
Lightening on the patio, the thin sun
Splintering on an inlet of grass. He's grown
Heavier even now. Just yesterday, he's sure,
He was *almost* 12. A fact, at 12, that's more
Like dream. A can of pop bobs half in
And out of the deep end before him. When
He raises, at last, both arms above his head,
The light floods from him in ragged threads.

The Moles

In this incremental darkening,
short, almost ratcheted turns of it,
his white trousers move over the lawn
as if of their own power. Summer,

years back: my father is tamping down
molehills, dowsing along tunnels
raised like skin above tendons, moving out
onto the high wire of decorum,

like a drunk performing for highway police,
his tasseled loafers indistinguishable from grass,
the beer and paper he'd gone to get
become his balance bar.

But he was a king to me. For him,
power lines drew taut, like violin strings
glinting across the hollow valley and our lawn,
newly patched, where the well had been drilled.

He was a king and 34, with half his school loans paid,
digging a hinged divot with his heel, calling me out
to help him bury a penny, proclaiming, one day
my boy would find it and become magically wealthy.

And what, exactly, did the moles make
of all this? That gift,
which has become the memory itself,
is a tunnel I nose through.

Our patio lit like a runway.
Insects of all kinds sparking

from the sides of that house.
Through his thin blue shirt, I could see

the dark of his body,
like a shadow on the moon,
like my mother watching from the kitchen,
her concern cast on the blinds,

and then the world was dark
and we were not going in.

The River

That fear inside me all this time,
the chicken wire I could almost see through to,
turns out to be just a childhood—
fully formed, but boyish,
wrapped in a blanket
within shouting distance
of the house he grew up in.
It's 3 o'clock in the morning,
the inside of black, blacker even
than the hair of the woman he'll later marry,
and all he wants now
is to be swallowed whole by sleep—
to sleep and add the sound of his breathing
to all the night sounds around him.
He has yet to realize his family
is part of the world and so he has renounced
with it the world and so he is sleeping
beside the night, not with it.
The sound of black does not yet run through him,
and no matter how black his sleeves,
the pale palms of his hands remind him
he is himself still, separate.
That stone in the brook,
like the knuckle of a hand—
is the river in it
the way he wants to be in someone?
He needs to think that,
splitting the stone, he would find its center
damp as the very late or very early mist
that finds its way into the heart and dissolves
its boundaries. He does not yet know
the mist takes its shape from the emptiness
of the world, it begins there

between trees and houses,
in the margins of singularity
that allow us to see each other.
He doesn't know the mist would mean nothing
were the world whole,
or that the world is whole because of the mist,
or that though one day he'll no longer see himself—
though that boy will seem no more to him
than a log softened by flame—
the rock, at its heart,
was wet with the river,
and the river flowing more slowly through rock,
was nonetheless a river for that.

A Stone

2000 miles and 10 years west, the key is still in my desk.
Keeping it served what purpose? Someone else now sets
their briefcase next to that door and unlocks it, entering
another day of what seems to be destiny, but is only
a life. Those years were a breeze that moved us,
mussing the long hair we braided into a semblance of order.
There is Brigid, on the lawn in a circle of students so eager
it hurt my eyes to look at them. Her death a stone
in her hand. Slender stone, charming, machine tumbled
and set in sterling, the chain has broken so she holds it
in her palm. There is too much weight to carry and not
wear down from futures we could not have imagined into
pasts we barely lived. It has to be remembered
to be realized, it has to be called up and burnished
by the present until the pure slick of eternity
shows its intricate grain. Newspapers line the bottoms
of moving boxes, using casually the names of varied dead,
as if the quilters still met Thursdays, as if the Ross twins
were still Mayor and Justice of the Peace,
as if the cheese factory had not long ago ceased
its smelly enterprise. The wind moves the trees, the gray
clouds shift along slipstreams, the students sprawl
in shade then sun then shade. Off again, on again lover,
the wind. When it was home, the whole campus
lightened, then it would be gone for days
and return so tired it could barely rustle leaves.
But even on gray days it created such a chorus of green,
such a silvering, it had to be taken in and embraced,
it had to be forgiven.

Sorrow Bread

The trees were backlit, like a Sunday school play,
and as the sun went down behind the quarry,
a spider made his way around and around
one leaf on a sapling next to them, playing out
the thread by which a spider keeps itself in the world,
drawing together that slick, green leaf
into an inverted cone meant to shed the coming rain.
The man thought of the carefully folded wax paper
they'd eaten their sandwiches from. He thought of each
crumpled piece relaxing back into a square
in the dark of the knapsack beside them.

Below, rings appeared on the water in the quarry,
and even after she felt the rain she claimed
it was a host of fingerling bluegill and bass, free now
to come up and mouth the cooling surface. "No,
that's rice," he said, "rice from heaven. Happy anniversary."

This took place in Indiana, which is a state I know well.
I know the woods and the quarries, and how it feels
to be walking in the woods and have the forest give way.
It delighted me, staring down into quarries.

The man and the woman sat at the edge for a very long time,
so that when they rose to go home, her legs had gone to sleep.
He put his arm around her, supporting her. She grinned
and said, "You must feel like this when you sit on the toilet
reading for so long." He was a minister. She was a nurse.
For a while, each looked at the smile on the other's face.
Then she said it was all right, they'd just have to move slowly.
And so he let go of her, reached down for their knapsack....

I painted bridges for a living once, and once

I felt my rigging tremble, and looked up to see
my partner falling away from me. I know that work
and what it feels like to walk into work with somebody
day after day. My partner loved to drink beer for lunch, sit
right next to the juke box and sing. He wanted to be a rock star

but he hit the ground on his side, like a little boy
who'd just been tucked into bed. And at the height
I watched from, the sound his body made seemed
a childish moan of regret, as if it were summer,
and too early to be dark.

What do you do when there's nothing you can do, but
you can't just do nothing? When you've coexisted easily
with time, and then, suddenly, there's no time,
followed by the flood of too much? It took so long
to get to him, each thud of my boots echoing
in the bottomlessness of my head.

Another time, I was holding a rope that snapped; no one
got hurt, but I remember holding onto that useless end
long after it looked silly to be doing so. On deep nights,
at least some of them, I dream I'm still there: flat
on my ass with my feet braced against the guardrail,
trying to live up to obligations that aren't valid anymore.
What am I doing but saving myself? Maybe
that rope tied to nothing was actually holding me up
during the long fall my soul took
as friends' heads swung from sight.
Maybe the all or nothing of it all
was working its way into my hands like a cramp,
making certain I'd never forget how easy dying is.

The nurse opened her eyes once and saw him weeping,
searching her wrist for a pulse. Perhaps she thought,

Now I know what I looked like to the people I cared for.

I knew none of these people, really. I never asked
if my young partner wanted kids, or what he would do
with a million dollars. The reverend and his wife led
the church of some old friends in Indianapolis, who told me
about the accident over the phone. But I was moved somehow,
and as I sat on the porch watching our spiders arrange
their nets in the shrubs, I began to see both incidents clearly.
And I saw the husband, hoarse from begging a forest for help,
have to choose between staying and going.

Rita came home then—after being in Connecticut for a day
and a half—wanting to play, say hello, and hold each other—
but I stayed where I was, circling the piece of paper
and these random events, until she turned off the lights
of the screened porch, trying to get a reaction.
I said "please" twice, then screamed, "I'm writing out here!"
so loudly that it echoed in the valley around us.
I moaned, *Why is she doing this? A thread like this only happens
once or twice a year.* How puny my voice must have seemed
to any neighbor; what a statement to have drift in
while you're washing dishes or reading the newspaper.

My partner survived and in two years was painting bridges again.
He lives in Missouri, which is, like Indiana, someplace
I used to think I knew well. The hospital nurses liked him,
because he was patient, and never complained
or was angry with them for doing their jobs.

I should stop this now, before the first few drops of rain
begin darkening the sill, and climb the slick stairs toward bed
where I know the woman I love is waiting for an explanation.
"It's me," I should say to the dog in the doorway, "I'll take it
from here." Then again, I would say anything to make myself
feel less helpless, to extract good from bad; I would say anything

to go on, and need to admit that outright.

I've tried hard, looking down at this rope, to love the knots
I slide down to, to see other hands than mine there;
but it is my rope and no one else's.
Everyone has their own rope, and each reaches the end
in his own sweet time.

Red Lead, 1978

The way a boy might kick a can,
or a field goal, or a stone to skip
down one long empty street
toward a home that held no warmth for him;
as if putting on a sock or unbuckling a belt,
some small gesture shared by all of us,
he kicked him in the face. Then,
standing like a hunter over his trophy,
one foot on the tailgate,
he dabbed blood from his boot
with a napkin.

Behind us, clouds muddied the horizon,
pigeons peered from their nests in the girders,
and the latticed shadows of the bridge
lay like a puzzle on the ground.
To the east, the broken-toothed St. Louis skyline
yawned up into haze. *It is a trial*, the stanchions
murmured, *bound here as we are, our sorrows given
so we won't float toward heaven too soon.*

Spot primer, finish coat, blood, dust and asphalt.
Squabs laid gingerly down to die
by bottle caps full of water. For miles,
that paper napkin rode the Missouri,
getting darker and darker, going under,
being pulled apart and into
the fierce, filthy river of everyone.

Cassandra by a Nose

The words won't match up with this music, Toots.
Scheherazade and *Helen*, neck and neck,
Eurydice dropping back along the rail. Seriously,

who'd choose an amplified bugle
to herald *Ophelia* on the infield,
or, from the shit-pocked, rose-petaled winner's circle,

Beatrice hoofing it toward her stall in hell?
Allusion doesn't jibe so well
unless there's mythic pain.

In an hour and 41 minutes, their planes
will taxi off in opposite directions.
The blood on his noggin will clot,

the lipstick on his collar will fade.
And as her half of a tear-stained wager stub
wafts to the bottom of her inscrutable purse,

the seedy gumshoe will arrive at the airport,
derringer in his fedora, but decades too late.
All this screenplay lacks is a finale grand enough

to fit all these egos in one frame:
the copper with his leathery (but principled) heart,
the dandy gambler oiled with silk,

the alcoholic former beauty queen
that each loves in his own selfish,
doomed, less than swashbuckling way.

What else is there to know?

A slender, irresistible throat
and four hands always this close

to throttling what they love.
Predictable plots. Casting to type.
Blanks in surplus weaponry

that actually killed men during the war.
Yet, for all this, we find noir real enough:
fresh milk bottles on the stoop,

bloated corpse on the porch;
the brunette ingénue in white,
the harlot bright blond as a torch.

Each, toward the end,
has a sultry voice and likes things rough,
and always, by its credits,

the thorn outlasts the rose
being flush can't buy you heaven
and it's *Cassandra* by a nose.

Better Homes and Gardens

Shot himself. Hanged himself. Shot himself.
Fell from a window just half washed.
Couldn't go. Couldn't stay. Hadn't the heart.
Stopped at a train crossing, then couldn't start.
Hit-and-run at the school bus. Lost five toes to an axe.
Hydroplaned east on a westbound road.
Took the whole vial hoping to relax.
Shot himself. Hanged himself. Starved herself.
Caught with a schoolgirl. Fell in the tub.
Turned to God. Jumped bail. Collapsed in Jim's Pub.
Heart attack. Down's Syndrome. Cirrhosis. Stroke.
Shot himself. Hanged himself. Strung out on coke.
Incest. Seagrams. Scarred for life. Broke.
Polaroids. Videos. Chat room trysts. Tapes.
Blacked eyes. Slashed wrists. Post-marital rapes.
Curious tots tied with duct tape and string.
These are a few of our favorite things.

Palm Springs

Bobsled of vanity, imploding casket
of leisure and skin cancer, autopsy table
of failed marriage and midlife crisis —
could the sun-gods, tracked by shadow and angle
across temple courtyards,

could they have imagined the tanning bed?
Or how, here, in the neon-drenched, operatic
hospice piano lounge of our world,
we worship selves we want, but cannot be —
intravenous drips of bile and self-pity —

until the transplant ice chest opens
and the bartender scoops out the heart,
offering it once more, in the name of love,
to the body? Can someone explain to me why,
once we have lain down in our self-made beds,

we choose to get up?
Why, having been divorced and jettisoned,
we insist on perking up again —
each flagellant helping his neighbor,
bringing, as it were, his expertise to bear —

until each visitor is escorted, sedated,
from the asylum ward, committed again
to line dances and speed dating?
Fountains of perpetual joy and anguish,
we are but skin poured forth,

caressed, and poured again:
the magician, whose wife has sawed
all he owned in half;

the physician whose husband has his ear
to the heart of the babysitter;

the field commander calling in the coordinates
of his own suburban home;
the voyeur cabbie, nibbling lettuce in his shell,
for whom dawn is a Dollar Store place setting
minus a beloved to breakfast with.

There are (and ever will be), for each,
the spa's pleasures:
crystal healing, mud masks,
the vaguely urinous hot mineral springs,
and, of course, the tanning bed—

that flaming stretcher
on which we are borne
narrowly along
each wanton trench
to glory.

Party of One

There is no single discernible conversation,
just a low-level radiation
of language, a mélange of night sounds;
separate timbres elbowing in,
then relaxing into the crowd
that saves each from responsibility.

Be it ranch style or at forty stories,
the tall windows steam
against the outer cold,
the great room slowly fills
like an aquarium;
and just as we begin to drown
in companionship,
someone opens a door
and we are all swept out.

Housewarmings, open houses, mixers, soirées:
if someone plants a kiss on your cheek
and a drink in your hand,
consider yourself blessed.
What are we when we have nothing to hold?
When our gesticulations don't result
in clicking ice or pretzel batons
conducting "Some Enchanted Evening"
for an audience of one?

And if someone, their hand cupped
derringer-like to the small of your back,
bulldozes you toward the blind date
of your dreams, so much the better.
Bless the hostesses of America!
Think of them fondling and stuffing

the jarred olives, making sure
each pimento is in the olive it loves!

Think of how the perfect crackers
float equipoised on their perfect trays
while their guests circle
the carcass of a cheese ball.

And then there you are
on the balcony, the portico,
the overhang, the minaret
of daily life! There you are
above it, yet in it. The wind
glides across you
like a hot oil massage
and you have been lifted up,
are being held up,
like a champagne flute
above the earth!

All those lights down there
and no one sees you.
All those cars and buses
and not one is on its way
to your house.

3. Barbells of the Gods

The Barbells of the Gods

It's a Thursday, getting late,
and we're the last three cars in the lot.
Richard has his face in his golf clubs
like they're flowers and smell nice,
and Buster is already talking bowling balls and shoes,
talking us slowly out of summer,
when Rich looks up sideways and says he's never been
with one man long enough to watch a pair of jeans fade
and what's it like being married to women?
Out on the lake there's that kind of silence that's loud—
two suns moving towards each other, one perfect, the other
just a glare—and I clean and jerk one last beer
and we talk about desire,
but nobody here, our legs dangling over fenders,
knows what he wants or how to get it any more
than when we were kids
and girls spent their adolescence as the hood ornament
of some boy's father's car. It's too
complicated, Buster says.
And he means the rule book is immense,
that there doesn't seem to be a clear point
or object to him.
But I say, you must have dreams of growing old
with one person
and how has it been so hard, pardon the pun,
no offense, to find the right guy?...
I did, Richard breaks in, but he's married
so that's kind of why I'm asking you.
And I say, oh,
and Buster says, let's go someplace noisy
where we can really talk

Lazaruses of the Links

Sometimes, I think I am having a stroke, he said, there is this rusted hinge in my head, this cat in heat who wants outside and a tornado siren no one will do anything about ... really, the other said, putting for bogey, because, myself, I have no energy anymore, I should be chipper, mornings, I should be resurrected, instead, I am torn like a page from the notepad of death, my life checked off as if it were a chore... do you hear that, he said, replacing the flag, someone is vacuuming, I'd know my old Hoover anywhere, he said, there is still some of my ex-wife in the filter housing, and Wichita and Detroit...you don't know what this helplessness is like, the other said teeing up, I am a child again, I want my parents back... Tinnitus, is what the doctor says, he said, I am not certain, I had to read lips, he seems to think that like old age it is an incurable phase ...I refuse to be a list, the other said, I am a story, I am complex and richly textured, my plot matters...a woman is coming in that bungalow, he said, addressing the ball...look, we can't just let characters appear and disappear willy-nilly, the other said, it's irresponsi- ble and callow, he said, I mean, one should miss a wife when they just up and go. Life is precious, even if it's a made up one... one must replace one's divots... one must stay on the cart path... one must let the young play through....

In the distance, the great umbilical fuse of the horizon started sparking and hissing. Give me your scorecard, he said, we will see who beat who.

The Angelfish

Every day at five, the beautiful angelfish stops
at this corner of the tank. He is patient
and knows the bartender will come
with his salt shaker of food.

Every so often he glances around to see
if a certain female angelfish has come in.

He thinks about how if I stare at a woman long enough,
she will either blush or not and I will either blush
or not. It strikes him that fish don't have much weather
to talk about and he wonders if I know my mouth
is opening and closing all the time.

Does he love her? Does she prefer another angelfish
in another section of the huge tank? Will he ever
be happier than this? The bartender sees him now
and smiles and puts his big face up to the glass.

Something dry, the angelfish says, *something very dry.*

Like a Simile

Fell into bed like a tree
slept like boiling water
got up from bed like a camel
and showered like a tin roof.
Went down stairs like a slinky
drove to work like a water skier
entered the trailer like a bad smell
where I changed clothes like a burn victim
drank my coffee like a mosquito
and waited like a bus stop.
A whistle blew.
Then I painted like I was in a knife fight for eight hours
drank like a burning building
drove home like a bank shot
unlocked the door like a jeweler
and entered the house like an argument next door.
The dog smiled like a chain saw.
The wife pretended to be asleep
I pretended to eat.
She lay on the bed like a mattress
I sat at the table like a chair.
Until I inched along the stair rail like a sprinkler
entered like smoke from a fire in the next room
and apologized like a toaster.
The covers did *not* open like I was an envelope
and she was a 24-hour teller
so I undressed like an apprentice matador
discovering bullshit on his shoes.

Simile at the Side of the Road

In photographs of our galaxy
it looks like someone's just finished
stirring us with a long wooden spoon
like someone has the lid in one hand
head bowed into the steam
trying to figure out what it needs

like when your car overheats
and you open the hood
awestruck
with self-conscious ignorance
on a forming universe
to fiddle with important-looking things

while to schmucks passing at 70
which of course is illegal for good reason
(since one envies them now)
it looks like Rod Serling just got a good grip on your hair
and is pulling your upper torso into the Twilight Zone

though you're still there
of course
the fact of which
three small children pushing each other around
in the backseat are incessantly reminding you
and though the neuroses hurtling through the back of your
    head
have had to dim their lights
lost as you are
in this complex archetypal assemblage
with grease on your hands

(knowing well it will soon be on your face

inspiring dreams of ninjadom and pillage
at Babe's Pre-Owned Cars)

but leaving the war goop and camouflage wallet aside
(never point a loaded flour sifter
unless you plan on using it)
and getting back to that nice homey
mm-mm good soup metaphor

you know that you will really be in it
if you're late for work again today
so you grate your teeth
try once more to rub the Parmesan from your eyes
and think

the whole point being
that the kid scribbling crayon on your interior
can't write notes for *you*
and it's this
not looking at the Milky Way slowly cooling and clearing
against the black backdrop of hood insulation
that makes you feel so small

Still Life with Motion

My colleagues, like water forever poised
against the hydrant's dome,
we spend our days charged with responsibility
and nothing to do.

How we'd welcome a fire,
a good five-alarm, passion-struck, high-rise blaze
reduced to silence and smoke
by the mere opening of our mouths.

Instead, we regress on
through abstruse emanating circles
toward our original belly flops
into the water of being.

Then, after a hearty harvest breakfast,
we're off to analyze the field
some poor slob's working in.

Wasn't there once a means
by which the parallel parking slots
of strained joy and hostility
could be maneuvered?
By which our multiplicitous lives
needn't be reduced to one?

The monoliths of our time are billboards,
our main streets, now thruways.
We upgrade and uproot,
we rent our U-Hauls and our Ryders,
we shift and pack and lift,
we dolly, we cart, and still
the limp duffle bags of despair,

the Samsonite Pullmans of delusion,
arrive before us, remain with us.

The manic organizing, the back sprains,
the newspapered goblets nothing gets drunk from,
the excruciating 12-steps to recovery
all of which lead down into childhood's basement
and the huge coffin-style freezer
one has to sell with the house.

It is unending, this struggle to become,
to praise, to exist
with the smallest shred of confidence.
The diesels back onto the docks,
the forklifts scurry,
moths the color of coffee stains
butt all night against fluorescent tubes,
and like rugs beaten out
over clotheslines left strung only for that purpose,
we retain few traces
of the lives once ardently enacted.

Our ex-spouses' handwriting is still on boxes,
what once held negligees, now holds light bulbs,
what once went in the study, is now stacked in the shed,
and the ruts left in the front yard
become drinking troughs for sparrows,
the worms rise into them,
the birds rise out of them,

and we are miles away, our headlights still burning,
our alternators begging for mercy,
our stomachs growling,
our bladders distending,

oh take care my fragile friends,
we all settle during shipping,

we are sold by neither weight, nor volume,
we are not insured for replacment value,
all that we have been
layered hastily into one body
and shipped through year after year
of couriers and agents,
handlers and operators,
a kind of Century 21 bucket brigade
that ends only in evaporation
and long after the fire's reduced itself
to silence and ash.

Emergen(ce) of Feeling

That rain falls on palaces and prisons
at the same time, I did not know to be true.
That the first thing in the morning *was* the morning,
was only a guess I made one night. That one twin
will literally see her own death,
well, it seemed logical enough. Some airbags deploy,
others are not so timely. There are things school children
should not see on the bus ride home. Trust your trench coat
implicitly. To hunt the deer in motel room paintings
is folly. If the attendant has the key,
you don't have to buy the franchise.
Barometers, too, will tempt the clouds,
but nothing real about the world can be seeded
or weighed with truck scales. If the white lines are broken,
you are not looking fast enough. Lightning is God
taking pictures of the victims. The present, like your elbow,
bends just one direction. The orange-handled carafe
is always more full; you won't like it either,
but when you drink it, sip pensively
and kiss the ring on your own hand. Majesty
appears in many guises. Ghosts spend an eternity
trying to pick up a fork. It's ok to mistake
a stranger's window for your personal drive thru.
All window glass will be digital by 2017.
Tears are the adapter. We wonder how we survive
our childhoods. The answer is: we don't.
Adjust mirrors. Proceed slowly. Merge with next
sentence drawn inland from the coast.
We are all bees on a flowered dress.
We are all flies on piano keys. We are all echoes.
Sometimes in unison. Which makes us happy.

Why is That Pencil Always Behind Your Ear

I lay soaking into the beach, getting whiter and whiter,
getting it wrong. I laid on the beach with a hotel
for a tombstone, trying to think of our country
as one big old house with the sea for a backyard.

Some other kids were shoveling holes everywhere
and their dog, which had been frantically planting his flag
on the shore, and which had finally given up all hope
of leaving some trace of himself, lay down too,
and waited for them to finish. So I knew

then why some are said to howl at the moon.
It *is* a sort of madness. It's being the only dog
on a long stretch of beach—with shards of a foreign life
jammed between the pads of your feet. No wonder

he took such interest, later, when the gulls lowered
like a mobile and he saw the single black crow
walking speechless among them. He must have thought,
Oh comrade, the stories we could tell each other.

Maybe it was a fugitive from justice. Maybe it was rich
and bored. Or maybe it was just a dreamer grown tired
of the dead in the road. I couldn't tell you. But
you've been lost, haven't you? And you, like me, may have
a piece of No. 2 lead in your thigh that has been there

practically forever. Sometimes at work I'll drop a tool,
and in the instant it takes to pick it up, I'll feel the ghost
of a pencil behind my ear. A small, insistent pressure,
perhaps a little like the bunching of a dog's ribs

just before it barks. Or the wind catching beneath

a folded black wing. It recedes, but doesn't go away.
And it leaves the T-shirts and the lime shorts,
the flip-flops and the togs and the toys, the blue jeans

with black thighs where we've rubbed our hands. As if
someone else's life had just receded, leaving you your own.
Which is why, though the point snaps again and again,
I have to keep doing this.

Now the light inches down that hotel's face like tidewater.
Shortly, the crabs can come out and be safe on their many legs,
the oysters can surface to try once more to spit out the pearls
that hurt so much. Oh comrade, the stories we'll tell each other.

The Pole

Some mornings it takes an expedition to get to the paper, some days it has to be enough just to sit down and stare at it. The Antarctic, I call it, the blank white Word screen of death and I am Scott, slaughtering my sled dogs and eating their livers to stay alive. While all the Amundsens of the world skip ahead to the award ceremony, I am trudging in a hallucinatory haze 96 km in the wrong direction hoping to find a polar bear I can kill and crawl inside of and whose blood-sopped turds, yum, can sustain me. Oh, I don't think so, Galway, but then maybe that is why I am not so serious a poet, maybe I don't go that extra 11 miles and eat my own doo–doo — hell, I can't bear to read it, let alone choke it down. But where was I? Oh, back to the tundra, where I am peering out over my frosted goggles looking for a subject when it occurs to me my subject is always poetry, and writing about poetry *is* similar to scarfing your own shit, so maybe this bear thing has something to it after all. You are out there, alone on the ice floes, subzero temperatures, chill factor off the charts, not a single speck of ink in sight. It is lonely here, the world has nothing to say to you, it has its back to you, conversing with someone famous and more talented, they are clinking glasses and sharing an anecdote over walrus pâté, but that's ok, it is worth it just to be here in the vicinity of the pole, even if it has cost you nineteen ponies, your sled dogs and three toes, you will feel a lot better once you get those wet things off and huddle around the Sterno. "Why I never," as my grandmother used to say, which translates loosely in current parlance to, "Hell no, I am not eating that thing." But you are old school, you know you have gotten exactly what you wished for. Amundsen would never have used Skidoos or Snow Cats, either, it just takes all the challenge out of freezing to death; there is nothing heroic about coptering in your doublewide and setting up a generator. You have to keep your tent to a minimum for the poetry to count for something, you have to sacrifice, for Christ sake, lose at least one digit, drink your own urine once in a while. So I guess I owe Galway an apology, I guess there really is nothing else to sustain you, just the hoary hide of poetry, you just have to keep going on what you produce and what we produce truly is mostly crap most of the time. But I don't want you to get the wrong impression of me, I am a happy guy, really, I zip up my parka and go to work every day. I explore the blank page with some degree of noble aplomb. I know what it is to have tusks of snot frozen to my face. Eventually you have to just stick a flag in it and call it a day, this is what is yours, this little plot of ice, beneath your frostbitten mukluks, and it is wasteland, granted, but it is yours and at some point you have to accept you're *there*. It can't matter that you are off by 200 feet, or if you are writing in circles in a whiteout, repeating yourself repeating yourself, you are doing the best you can with the gear you lugged with you—here, have a herring.

Arf Poetica

For years, it will seem you've been abandoned,
in a great house with countless rooms,
while a grandfather clock
chips away at the immensity —

and it's as if a dog, some small breed,
perhaps shih tzu or terrier,
refuses to stay still,
it will be whining or scratching or pouncing —

there will be salesmen at the massive door,
or a package you have not ordered,
or there will be engines revving,
with the savagery of lust or war —

and the little dog will look to you,
it will be afraid, then hungry, then thirsty,
it will be desperate for you to hear,
for you to look up, to *see* it —

and then to prove it has been noticed,
it will need to feel your fingers rub its temples
or the bridge of its flaring, wet nose,
it will have you believe

you can never turn back to what you were doing,
it will bark, turning circles, if you try,
it will make you feel that you are responsible
for that smaller heart, so much like your own,
beating twice, three times as fast as yours —

and even after you have pushed back from your desk,
even after you have picked the dog up from the floor,

and it is burrowed against you,
warm and with its head at last relaxed on your thigh,

you will feel that steady, wild heart at work,
the miniature lungs emptying and filling,
you will feel its submission offsetting fear —

and then, having learned that you are alive
and for the moment safe, sheltered, seen,
once it has taught you how small you are
and how much you depend on something
larger, more steadfast, more insistent within you —

then you must be able to write,
directly, honestly, fiercely, with one hand,
while all along soothing the dog with the other,

and if you can sustain this freely,
every day and for long enough,
poems will come without calling,
and you can den with grace among them
for the rest of your life.

4. Fugitive Love

Where

This last time I am touching you tentatively,
then withdrawing awed, as the first worms
to find our bodies will. I am looking
for happiness and sadness,
the invisible kingdoms where they reside.
A people in New Guinea claim that intellect
lies in the larynx and that only in voice
is the truth known. We speak
of the heart, the navel, the portholes of our eyes,
but today I am thinking with my fingers,
remembering the first woman to guide them,
and the fact that she has three children now
while I have none, and that after so many years without
an *accident*, I have to doubt I ever will.
Your breasts are like drifting clouds, I see
something new in them every time you breathe.
But they are not where the happiness is.
Your abdomen is a series of hills. Yet that, also,
is not where happiness is.
Your hand is a white horse, perfectly satisfied
to pull quietly at the darkening grass.
The blue vein in your thigh is where it drinks.
And the artery pulsing nearby
is the rest of the herd terrified
into the canyon of my hand
where the sadness will be tomorrow.

Geese

We were in love and his uncle had a farm
where he took me hunting
to try to be in love even more.

He wanted me to have what he had:
pitch black coffee,
toast buttered with bad light

in a truck stop splotched with smoke,
then moonlight over hills of snow
like a woman stepping out of her dress.

And it was nice even as we killed it—
the stalks lightening, the sun rising
like a worn, yellow slicker

over us, bent over panting
because it wasn't shot cleanly
and had run us both dizzy

before settling down.
There was a hawksbill knife he used
to make the anus wider. After that,

one could just reach in
and remove what wasn't necessary,
and thinking about it now, I see

the school desk behind his uncle's barn
set there for that reason,
see my husband sadly hosing it down,

as if regretting how and what

men are taught...
I'm lying...

Though the diner I see belongs
in a small town where I went to school,
the desk had no drawers, was in fact a table,

and he was whistling as he washed it.
The sun didn't rise
like something to keep the rain off us;

it hung, like a cold chandelier
in which I could see each filament
in each flame-shaped bulb

beating itself senseless against the light—
brilliant and hollow,
beautiful and inhumane...

But I wanted so badly
to forgive his hands,
forgive his lovers,

and to forget how, driving home,
I was fooled by half an acre of decoys
and some camouflage netting,

how I wanted to honk but didn't,
and how the whole scene made me realize
that mannequins mate for life too,

in department store windows,
wearing Sunday-best clothes,
that if you press hard enough

on a bird's dead breast,
it will betray its own kind,

that when he wrung its neck and broke it,

I sighed his first name.

Compass

This table between them, he thinks, can be said
and will be, not the something else. This
and not that, this and no other. To him,
the narrow window seems a specimen slide,
a cross section of the world. Does one
look out or in to look down? To her,
the rectangle of light is another, special box
among the boxes. Light as a Styrofoam cup,
she could blow away. What keeps him here
is the unsaid weighting his legs, the mass
of two donuts in the wax-lined bag, the fact
that she's listening. Fifteen years funneled
to this five minutes, the way, sometimes,
when it first rains, the first drop
carries the whole sky in it. She fidgets,
she's so weightless, the air so thick
with meaning, she knows that the *this*
has passed, that they can only decide
what to give back. He's always been
arrogant, he's always believed in his word,
but now the little tea not gone
is cold to his lips. He can't open them
to drink, let alone speak. In March
of last year's insurance calendar,
the cattle, their necks scarred,
keep to the center of their pasture,
ankle deep in the softened ground.
Where anger has been swallowed,
it must be spat out; if it cannot
be brought up, it will have to be re-invented.
But for now, all this waits inches down
the road map in his glove box. It's this
place, this sagging square yard of linoleum

on which the unplugged refrigerator upholds
its open doors. It's what wells
in the shared plastic spoon between them,
the one that will be on the table for years
after the chairs are pushed back empty beneath it.

X Marks the Spot

At fifty, the perfect storm,
Front into front.
The capsized hull, one's own face.

And to speak across, each from each,
An attorney's table—
The arduous stripping
Of marriage's wet clothes.

The tide of digits carried forward.
Flotsam of ill-will and regret.
A resentment that has looked to us
For sustenance, a persistent pet
Rubbing its length against pallid ankles.

Was that our vows sucked like smoke
Into the air ducts? Our punctuation's last mark?
Each compromise slips precisely over others,
The fluid, age-old lingerie of schooling sharks
Coaxed from submerged ruins.

The equator's curve completes itself.
The napkins lie crumpled.
The table will be round long after
Each gender assents
In civil and unanimous discontent.

What couple ever does this well?
One finishes the complimentary strudel.
One signs at the X one is—
Here, here and *here.*

Divorce

Like deeply chained buoys, languid and backlit by a neon sign,
they're still dancing to slow ones in the rear of the bar.

Old friends, as you said, come here to "do drinks," throw darts
and "connect" with each other,

couples who have the feel of having known each other
for "longish" times,

before this place got popular with younger crowds.
Not old, of course, most aren't much older than you and I,

but still, with that weathered, companionable look
that marriage gives you

and five daiquiris can't take away—
like that tie you loosened, but could not bring yourself to undo

so you just slipped it over your head twice a day. And if now,
in the john, you're thinking, *Well, yet another glass raised*

against end-rhyme and Love's tailored, dry-cleaned noose;
another zipper lowered on upwardly mobile values,

how do you explain that I've never seen you look so lonely
in your whole half-life as a moment ago,

slipping past that bald guy—whose cigarette, incidentally,
you put out with your coat—playing darts back there,

dancing simultaneously and cheek-to-cheek with a wife
who'll need surgery to get out of her clothes?

One slow turn and he'll aim, then throw the third and last,
then gently pat her ass

until she unlocks her arms, lets him go out a channel
between the pretzels and ivory-colored drink

she holds in respective hands.
For your birthday, all you wanted was to get to the bathroom,

and were making headway, until our waitress drove you against
them. And him, he swayed a little, then caught again

on the rhythm, reached down between their chests for matches
and craning his head behind hers re-lit the stub in his mouth,

while, as if you'd caused some immeasurable disturbance,
seeming to hold her even tighter for a moment,

dancing her away and toward the round and tortured board,
not wanting to know if there was a hole in your life or not,

a black smudge to remember as meaning
one shouldn't, but has to, get close to love as that.

Joyland

Here, between teen lovers spooning each other ice cream,
and the press of a five-putting family of four,
along the unraveling carpeted fairways
to Rapunzel, Snow White and Sleeping Beauty
there will be no playing through.

Soon lights will appear
in the windows of the windmill,
the tree house, the coastal beacon.
Soon the synchronized fountains will fall and rise
reminding us it has always boiled down to precision timing

and score cards that tell us little
about those myths by which we've lived.
That mini-villa, is that the famed artists' colony,
snow painted on its roofs, tinsel icicles dripping from its eaves,
spiritual haven for the single or soon to be divorced?

Beside you and your silent wife,
on the surface of the man-made lagoon,
its waters laced with blue food dye,
a real rain begins to fall, rings appearing,
as if invisible range balls were plunging from heaven.

There is, at the heart of the matter,
some wiring, a weak motor and a two 60-watt bulbs.
Sure, the little drawbridge goes up and down
and the moat indifferently returns each ball to your instep,
but you know what's going on

behind the saloon's teensy swinging doors;
you should have been able to say no, should have
returned your watch warm to your wrist

and your keys to your hand,
and the ice bucket, unused,

to its plastic tray on the toilet tank.
And it doesn't matter whether she knows or just suspects,
you have felt the pointed tap of her putter
square on your heart saying
nothing will ever be the same.

Smoke chuffs from the teepee.
A few leaves curl at the igloo door.
You could swear you saw a field mouse in the chapel's spire.
Meanwhile, your wife is perfecting her stance,
aligning her shoulders and feet, distributing evenly

the new weight of having smelled another woman
on your clothing. Let the warning lights of the water tower
blink off and on all night, let the planes traverse the sky,
there are these holes you have dug for yourselves,
this emptiness that need be aimed at, filled.

The Chair of Forgetfulness

My friend Karin,
tendering an emblem for her parents' divorce,
selected a possession they fought *to get rid of,* not keep.
A massive Victorian piece the entire family

had come genetically to dislike—
part chair, part umbrella stand, part coat rack, cedar chest,
  and mirror,
the individual accessories and clothings layered into strata
of warmth and thickness, pockets of color—

it loomed in the foyer
with a kind of mutant efficiency,
coming to embody all each didn't want in someone else,
all the inarticulate hope and sorrow

of merging and synthesis.
If Rodin had sculpted Hell's Chair of Forgetfulness,
it would have looked like this thing:
part electric chair and part throne, she said. And

I didn't hear the rest, indeed, I was off and running
thinking of how my own parents split,
pushing off as if each saw the other
as the side of a pool—then noting clinically,

how that leap made complete sense,
in the same way one wallpaper recalls another;
the general pattern
sparking on the stark screen of memory,

its brief fuse an afterglow
tracked back to the fossilized source.

Flora, fauna, all manner
of geometric and human shape,

which themselves extend further,
the way morphine extends the needle,
into brief trace flashes, recognitions
of even the most innocuous places:

Tastee Freezes; five-and-dimes; church bazaars:
parts of our daily, family *being-ings*,
a forgotten world that required soup and support hose—
the world before a satchel became a briefcase,

and the coffee filter basket filled each morning
with a fresh burial mound of dirt,
and there was Death, that slight ring of lipstick
now glazed on the cup rim

the way reality always camps on the edge of a good time,
so that the firelight just fails to illuminate its face,
so that eventually you find yourself
a weakening concentric circle

thirty-seven years from the stone,
in a lake you can neither drown in nor drink from,
like those water bugs who learn to worship the surface
as quietly as possible,

like those stupid flies you've witnessed trying to live on
  flowered wallpaper,
or, waking to find one on your face,
think, yes, it makes sense,
I've been dead since moving in here.

The Briefcase

They bought it early in their courtship,
at one of the estate or moving sales
they avidly frequented, assembling a life
from the treasures and trash of other couples—
young then, oblivious, able to profit
from others' losses, to foresee utility,
if not beauty, in the discarded and worn.

"Contents a mystery," the tag said,
"Combination unknown." Even so, it was
a bargain—a sleek, hard-shelled executive attaché,
its four dials frozen at 0299, the apex of ennui
at which someone quit trying.

Even recounting this story, he aches
with methodical, sequential tedium,
feels the dream overcome by drudgery,
the way their dinged muffin tins, bent whisks
and Jell-O molds signified dissolution
of their every merged ingredient—
became, finally, intractable result,
which, like good children,
they shut up and ate.

When it finally clicked open at 9898,
all he found within was another tag,
one that showed the combination he now knew,
and directions for customizing that code,
making it their own,
for which, obviously, it was too late,
there being nothing left
of their early hope to entrust there,

that trapped air of possibility
belonging, now, to others—perhaps you two,
parking on their weed-ravaged lawn as you have,
walking arm in arm up the drive
toward the warping, heaped card tables
and the garage door propped open
with a brand new broom.

Fugitive Love

Fused this way, naked and back to back, wrenched
in and out of love, he could be trying to say something,
she could be trying not to listen. It seems

important to know and I don't;
I doubt even Rodin did and anyway,
times like that, to say anything

is to say too much.
I think Rodin saw them as twins,
Siamese and fraternal, connected

and yet not. Longing
for more and less of the same.

At the cafeteria today, I saw two lovers
forget to pick up trays. They were so involved
with everything they didn't expect anything.

*

Opposite me, on the other side of the sculpture,
another man and another woman. I can't tell
if they're together really. How long, or if,

they've known each other at all.
The look in his eyes is the look of a man
who has come a far way to say something simple—
Mouth half-open, eyes half-closed—

and I'm trying to imagine them like this forever,
just their clothes touching,
and how it will feel for them in the back of the taxi

that even now may be moving across the city.

Maybe the seams of their pants legs will touch
or the sides of the soles of their shoes.
And one will think, *please touch me so I can leave.*
And one will think, *please don't touch me so I can leave.*

Outside—a harsh light all over everything,
buildings rippling in their lustrous skin,

*

and someone else might call it Fear
and someone else *the tearing and merging of clouds*

but this has everything to do with her.
There are times when that's the way it goes with souls.
Back to back. Fruitless.

There are moments when the soul
seems more physical than the body, no one hears anyone
and saying anything is just a bronze scream.

And maybe this is what the man
in the sculpture is feeling and why he looks
as if he's boiling alive in the air around them
and why I don't think he's trying to speak at all.

Dunes

Despite the curvatures adapted each to the other,
The slackening skin that in sleep feels lost without that other's;
Despite the slatted fencing that marks their yard from others',
And the offspring at play within, their testament to others;
Despite all the others they have embraced and refused;
Despite all otherness between them
They've acknowledged and excused;
They can no longer in mystery come to each other,
With the quickening and total surrender to another
That both empties each and fills the other.
And so they go on, because each goes on, despite the other:
To each their own wind-ironed waters,
To each their own bruised sky and horizon,
Their own shames, their own redemptions,
Awakening to each night's newly shifted sloping,
Each day by unremitting day's abiding,
Without need for another day or lover,
They endure side by side, in their time, no other.

Meridian

Night out of day
Day into night
That first marriage
  One horizon
Back to back
One fused spine
  Yet their faces
Dusk and dawn
Turned toward
Each other's
Vanishing
  Glances
Traded sidelong
  What can be
Shared
To rest assured

        Love
We are still here
My ocean
Your shore
  Neither merely
Extension
Of that other's
Otherness
  How we know
Who we are
Upon waking
To either
Darkness or light
  Depending

Rubbing Dirt from My Dog's Nose, I Realize

I'm not crazed with loving, I don't see you
whenever I close my eyes, anymore.
When I think of us, it's like looking at my shoes
through a glass coffee table—
if I can reach the laces at all,
I tie them in another world
and my first thought is whose hands are those?

I don't see my own face, even
when my nose is scarcely an inch
above the glass,
and I can lean back then,
blunt my cigarette in the ashtray,
and remain completely alone.

I remember the snow though, can you?
In another hour or so, we knew, it
would be pushed to the sides of the road
and piled there to freeze and melt and freeze
so that it would hurt to have to walk through that snow again,
to remember it now.

Knowing that, all I wanted was for you to say
you saw the same things I did:
how the sparse weeds bristled at the base of the hill,
and how the snow seemed to fall in front
of the town below us,

like in one of those low-budget films
where each actor knows just how badly things are going
but keeps doing his or her job, listening
to the pre-recorded barking
of dogs that have been bones for years,

and the muffled scrape of snow scoops long since
curled up into rust.

It was so still and yet you had to tell me
when I dropped my keys.
Pine trees leaned into each other and
their branches touched the ground.
A squirrel jabbed its head into the snow.
By afternoon, there would be so much
that people getting off work would have to guess
which car they held the key to.
In the same way that when I close my eyes now
I can almost miss even the idea of you.

I just realized I've never actually seen my dog bury anything
at all, but squirrels do and certain species of tree feel gratitude
when they forget just where.

It's the same sort of difference
and forty years from now
that's probably all there'll be to it:
I'll look at snow and fill with something that's just like snow,
one flake will land between my hair and my collar,
and I'll have to lean against who's near me.
It's how I'll stand not even having you to bear.

5. Fatherhood

Sill

On the kitchen sill,
in the square brick house
my aunt aged and died in,
the flawless hand-blown pear
will neither rot nor last.

My daughter, too young
to ever think of this again,
once took it down
and placed it in a bowl,
with the breakfast oranges.
She'd thought it lonely, I guess,
with just the sunlight against it,
that single breath,
exhaled, perhaps, just after lunch,
smelling of cheese and peach schnapps.

Dust is the pollen of our dying,
even children sense this,
and after she'd wiped it clean
with her flowered dress,
she held it suspended
by its delicate, disproportionate stem
and lowered it into the wooden bowl.

Her great-aunt, though,
had little patience with disorder,
couldn't bear the clean, unblemished outline
where it had originally been,
and that was that.

Moments ago, after assurance that her family
would all recognize each other in heaven,

my daughter asked who would take care of her things.
And when I said her babies could, she cautioned
that babies can't even take care of themselves.

Neither can we, of course, never quite tall enough
to reach the light switch, never quite able to drink
from the wall-mounted fountain of contentment,
we stuff our pockets with beads and bottle-caps,
we organize our knick-knacks as best we can.

My aunt's squat, miniature tract house was razed.
Her window sill exists only in the heaven of children.
The pear, it could be anywhere,
like the last breath of the old German who made it.
Likewise, her porcelain salters
and the hummingbird still hovering
at its glass flower.

Make the Cobra Talk

Some mornings, if his breathing is light enough,
if the lengthening light corresponds
to the angle of his sleeping,
I can see the face of his death
just beneath the surface —
narrowed, gaunt, *every hair in place*
as my grandmother used to say —
not five, anymore — a blonde flame
teased by bad dreams and night sweats,
springing up, as if deer had lain on him
for the whole of a night —
rather, the resilience spent, his dying
a kind of outage, the unpredictable
power pole downed blocks away,
the predestined rupture
of a pipe below the street.
In my office, on my desk,
on page 53, in Berg's poem "Page 256,"
Kafka says *We struggle with dream figures,*
but our blows fall on living faces.
Meantime, my son yawns hugely,
a kind of pull-chain he can reach
that blocks the horns and sudden braking
of traffic on the street,
refuses to be tucked in completely,
surrounds himself with rubber snakes,
and boasts *I'm stronger than myself,*
a moment of twisted bravado
that makes perfect sense to me
after a long day of being bossed around
by superiors and clients,
and so, when one hand creeps
from the covers, and he says *Make the cobra talk,*

I hear dew inch down grass stems,
the sirens twist like screws from green wood,
and say *I am not good, but I do love you,*
and I will coil with you all night.

At the Crematorium, My Son Asks Why We're All Wearing Black

These days the system is state of the art—mere scrims
of smoke, no odor. At least the neighbors don't protest
and the birds still gather on the tarred roof's edge
around seeds pooled at drain tiles. We accumulate
and are dispersed at the traffic light out front,
while within this relay point of caskets and morgue lockers,
the husks of our fallen continue their diminishment.

We're all members of this committee, son. We serve
with our tanks full and our tops down
until in one moment
we are reduced to manila envelopes
of movie stubs, bus transfers and address books;
in another, to pollen ruffling
the overcast, distended cloud cover of the world.

The passing lanes, the turn arrows,
the no U-turn and school crossing signs,
they all lead here.

You're old enough, now, for one dark suit and tie—
and to know exactly why
you're uncomfortable wearing it.

Get Me Again

My son-to-be schools in sleep
amongst his creatures of the sea—
Tootle Turtle, Dork-The-Dolphin, a killer whale
too new to have been named. He's been learning

to swim—we inflate his water wings,
and he becomes a toddling god,
launching himself out
into the deepest part.

And though his whole life
has been tense with waiting—
a fluid rippling in its container
as men walked by—once,

after we'd slipped off his floats
and were about to go home,
and he'd stepped over the edge
straight down to the drain,

I heard him boast
"I have been to the bottom of the pool,"
as if he'd planned it.
This fascination with water—the instinctual

fear and drive to be immersed—to what
can we attribute it? Today,
I found the calendar my ex
planned our life with

before it ended. Just two years past,
yet I struggled to place her
handwriting. Isn't it wondrous

how whales can speak

when hundreds of miles apart? He
seems to fear that I'll move away.
Twice this week, he's asked
my brother and sister's names,

where are my mommy and daddy.
I can't convey the placid stun
of this new family next to me.
What he knows? I drift in with donuts,

get to hold his mother's hand. Evenings
we play the game
in which bath toys cruise his sea, saying
"I'm just a lonely shark, please pet my nose,"

and though I say fish falling for that deserve
to be eaten, time and again
he falls for it. It is all about
surprise and predictability—

the predictable unexpected that children understand.
And don't we all know what's going to happen?
And aren't we surprised when it does?
The sea grass knows—always bending to the sea,

it has the barest of selves to hide in. "Bitter, bitter,"
warns the sea urchin, "this is how I taste,"
and when one self meets another and is afraid,
it says "bitter" also.

But this is always a posture, isn't it?
Because we want to be swallowed
as long as we're swallowed whole.

I like to think of my parents holding each other in the dark—

I like to think of their hair becoming the same color
and her vocabulary becoming his—the two repeating
each other's words, just to hear them again.

"I have been to the bottom," he bragged,
once his awkward body was no longer racked with coughing,
once his mother's towel had dried him.
But, at bedtime, fear having opened his eyes
to the water, he whined,

"If my ceiling flickers one more time, you're fired."
Meaning: "turn off the tv so you'll hear me when I need you."
Meaning: our little goldfish faces us, no matter what;
inside the one-gallon aquarium of the self,
hungry beyond all sense, it mimics our mouths

and like commuters in separate vacuum sealed cars,
it lip syncs love songs and frustrations
we've ceased to know. The way our children—
those mini-versions of ourselves we're free to love—
snort and snuffle in distant rooms, asleep so deeply
they could only be wide awake.

Dark Black

Indelible, less color
than psychic stain,
something so ancient and pervasive
it has become the norm
there at the tightened corners
of great-great grandmother's mouth,
the browning daguerreotype photo
behind smudged glass.
At what level is clarity struck?
In which generation do the masks become faces,
do my children put aside
their darkness on bed stands
and see, not endings,
but beginnings
in themselves?

Last night, an hour after I turned off her lights,
I heard my daughter sobbing.
Her goldfish was dead,
the story's step-mother was mean,
some boy had pushed her down at school.
There was no rest there, in the dim light cast
by her porcelain lamb—
she could not let herself sleep.

How did it first enter me?
Wading the asphalt? Walking
the creek bed's putrid shore?

Dark black, she says, when asking
her brother to hand her a crayon,
the deepest one, the one
that is like looking down a well

far past sadness and decay
into the lustrous reservoir of carbons and clay.

For as long as she lives,
she will be that wick,
burning, blackening, drawing
upon the deep oils of beginnings and ends;
all she knows but does not know she knows.

Fatherhood

Your life will be half-over when you arrive
at this porch yourself, the stars close and clear
through your breath, the moist, misted breath
of the one world we all contribute to, fully present,
quivering with distances. And if the back-light
from your kitchen door throws a skewed rectangle
into which you fit like a coffin,
know that I'm behind you then, helping you
not to lie down, helping you to stand straight up,
taking in the blades of cold, going on and on,
though your body stays rooted firmly
at the edge of all you've built.

Once my dirt is turned, your gardening begins,
and so I offer this soil I didn't know I was making,
this darkness from which flower light arcs,
perennial, inextinguishable,
spearing all with beauty.

Drive the trowel deep, separate the ribs,
tamp far into me your guilt and shame. I will
no longer be separate from you then, together
as we could not be while I lived. We'll be as lilies
sprouted from the same bed, having gouged out our place,
now bowed with rain, now upturned and listening.

And I will be with you on your father's rounds,
this late, when the only sound is your neighbor's heat pump,
and the hanging plants twisting on their chains,
once you have been compelled back into the house,
floorboards shifting beneath the carpet.
The nightlight in the children's bathroom
glows on the bath toys in the hall—

nothing has been put back,
which means all is where it ought to be,

and the children, breathing arduously after a long day
of touching everything they own at least twice,
seem to have fallen from jungle gyms
into their beds, their lips dry when you kiss them,
their faces cool, their hearts rhythmic in some dream place.

From one room to another in the house of yourself,
surprising a silverfish, straightening frames,
repositioning your wife's pillows on the stained couch;
that's how I see you, turned inward, finally,

having acquired something to lose,
a shadow in boxer shorts bending over the sleepers
with the weight of fatherhood
like a sleeping newborn on your chest,
her ear to your heart.

Soon you will turn even deeper into the house
and the warmth of a woman who will forgive your absence
if only you turn fully and to her alone.

Just a little while longer, you'll think,
then I'll go to bed,
just one more moment
and perhaps they'll smell your skin, sense you there
perhaps dream of you watching over them,
doing what you can to see the darkness for what it is
to leave it outside pressed against the windows,
leaning in its turn, over all of you.

Want

Kiefer, sweet boy, too far from me now,
the bobber dips so rarely in this life,
it's our job to be watching when it does.

Remember how brilliant and terrified
the little trout seemed, held up on your hook?
The gasp of joy it gave you?

Stop hiding, for a moment, whatever you've collected
in my shoe or your pillow case,
stop and listen this once.

That stone, greened with moss,
too big to be carried home,
is called a mountain.

You can sleep with the world for a while,
but then you have to put it back.

To My Daughter, Turning 16

Five construction paper apples,
our weathered familial orchard on a fridge door,
and with this opening of the freezer,
your photo's flowering fall to earth. So it is,
even thirteen years and a dozen states between,

you are plunked once more,
among crayons on that Kansas kitchen's tile,
savoring Bugles from your fingertips,
each in order, too intent to smile,
even as I picture you half in tousled bed sheets,

half in Sunday light: your favorite
mug dampening the classifieds;
a slice of toast smeared with honey;
the muted tones of a husband
humming in the shower...

Yes, I know, newsprint will be gone,
It's probably a wristband, thin as paper,
that projects the stories wherever you want...
still, tell me it's not too much to ask,
a father for his daughter:

the bedroom window of her own home,
a man who has loved her
more than he loves himself,
strong coffee,
some digital coupons to save,

while somewhere a windfall of apples,
after weeks of rain,
settles on the grateful grass
of an old man's grave.

Being Here

One day, you will visit me and find
I have returned to this time. Grown,
with children of your own,
you will kneel at my wheelchair or bedside
while I check your homework,
praise your grades. By then,

I will have forgotten enough days
to know clearly which mattered most,
and into those moments I will choose
to admit myself—recasting all,
recounting all, as I wish.
By then,

I will have shed all knowledge
of your mother's love for another man.
I will have tunneled through
the blame we cast and lay beneath,
solid years of it,
blind, deaf, rigid as a heap of stones,

through the threats and bickering over custody,
brief holiday embraces, the exhausted calm
after keening, once decisions have been made.
You will come bearing
your own evolving grief and betrayals,
the hard labor of becoming elders,

the frustrations of parenting and livelihoods,
your fears, fatigue, infatuations,
but I will see only your peaceful faces
against clean pillowcases,
your bedroom's deepening well of light,

your quick laughter at, and forgiveness of, each other.

You, who may not be speaking to one another,
whose spouses may dislike each other,
whose children may distrust each other,
whose accounts are overdrawn,
whose credit is over-extended,
whose fears out distance your faith,

I will remind you, from my pellucid dream,
how simple our journey really is,
how the gift of just being here
is worth any risk.
But I will say it with a young father's voice,
wistful, parting his children's curtains,

asking:
What are you hungry for?
Where do you need to go?
Will this make you happy?

6. Linda's House of Beauty

Running My Fingers through My Beard on
   Bolton Road

I've been thinking about the women who've kissed me,
I've been thinking a lot about them, and I've decided
that my mouth is nothing to be ashamed of. Like when
I mow the lawn and uncover the old elm stump we put
back in the ground. We said it was to help us split
the rest of the elm, but knew it was a sort of homage.

What goes around comes around, is one way of saying it.
Another is to answer, "Yes, you are pretty and I want you,"
after seven years, even though I say it
into another woman's ear. My beard has heard

all this before. The messiness of that hunger,
the memory of it. Sometimes it seems white
in the light I wake up to, but I am a young man,
something I tell my old dog when he's acted badly,
a horrible thing to say, "I will outlive you." Maybe, maybe not,
but probably

destined to. The way the way the papergirl hugged herself all
winter could not hold back her breasts. I watched her trudging
through those months in an adolescent stupor and I loved her,
wanted to bring her galoshes and tell her that one day
she would wake up and reconcile with this neighborhood,
and walk about freely in her memory of it
with nothing to deliver but her sweet, sweet self,
and that then she'd maybe smile a little,
remember how I always ran the stop sign
just as she had three more houses to go and...

But then spring sprang and I found my car veering toward her,
as it does toward exotic, beautiful other cars, and for a second, I

didn't love her really, just *wanted* somehow, and was ashamed.
Or did I? Was I? I don't know. There are so many men out here,
waiting to be saved from the awful shapelessness of the air
   around us.
I for one, cannot tell you how much I need breasts, and mouths,
and questions like the ones you asked me. I can't explain

the way my mother and my father's mistress coexisted
behind the buttons of your shirts. Or how I can close my eyes
and see the hay-yellow light of evening on my grandmother's
self-conscious face. How, though that newly raised barn is gone,
though the fiddle music which was just beginning
is gone, though every person who was there is gone, still,
a soft-faced boy raises one foot and begins to step toward her.

Child or woman. Memory or need. Today, again, I can see you
in her eyes, today her eyes again pursue the ground, look
for some sign, some path to follow away from her route.
Her sweatshirt is zipped to the throat and I am realizing that we
are both now, somehow ashamed of what's suddenly happened
between us. And I'm slowing down a little, as if to let
the spring sun catch up to these hands on the steering wheel,
to these hands that will not ever stop needing breasts to
make them hands, as if to uncover my mouth
and yell across the lawns to her.

It's wrong to not know how beautiful you are.
I shouldn't make too much of this, but all month
I've passed a boy in Vernon. He has track shoes slung
over his shoulder and cigarette smoke trailing out of his mouth,
like he'll never make up his mind.
It should come as no surprise, but he *is* walking south.
And there is something he has to ask you.

Morning Blend

She glides the cramped apartment kitchen, barely
clothed, spirited and graceful as a kind of animal,
with none of the night before's awkwardness,
the tentativeness, the brushings and nudges,

the shy gestures of a blossoming willingness,
until finally there was the naked union
of two imperfect truths and her perfect
twenty-something body poised above yours.

Now, this morning, there is the spatter of eggs
in the skillet, the scent of browning toast in the air,
and through one narrow, open window
waft sounds of the waking city, vibrant,

alive with small tensions, distant car horns
and street voices, an agitated dog
from the park across the way.
The two of you are comfortable for the moment,

being a man and being a woman, being alive together,
occupying the same century, neither wanting more
nor less than the other, neither asking questions
the other is unable to answer. It is so simple. It is all

as simple as this cup of coffee, isn't it? Of course,
coffee is not simple. Someone must grow it,
and harvest it and ship it. Someone must roast
and process and package and price it,

bearing, all along the way, daily traumas and trials
as they shuttle those beans to us. So, no, nothing is simple.
But lucid, yes, clear and unadorned, as the carrier,

the container for all this memory would convey to you.

What such a memory might mean to her, you cannot say.
Maybe it is as strong a force, maybe it is stronger.
Perhaps she has forgotten completely
that Brooklyn morning so long ago,

she who never seemed to notice her own beauty,
her own especial nature. Perhaps you were memorable
as a man, shirtless and in jeans, hair tousled,
slicing the fruit, tending the two cigarettes

in the ashtray on the table.
You cannot even remember now what caused
the disenfranchisement, the eventual detachment,
some difference, undoubtedly, in expectations,

some degree of disillusionment. Familiar bodies
came to seem foreign, trust wavered, interest waned.
But it could have as easily succeeded. One moment,
one defining moment of either sorrow or happiness,

one indelible shared experience could have been enough
to bond you two for life. We are always, it seems,
just a breath away from ecstasy or misery, take
your pick. It is, to some degree, chance that will decide

our fate, but then, you can finally accept that, now—
now that each of you is somewhere else,
now that the past is no longer to be reckoned with.
Your faults known and accepted fully.

Your aspirations revised by the acceptance of your losses.
Left to breakfast on what memory serves you, this
encapsulated joy of having been a young man: a lithe
woman in your white dress shirt, unbuttoned to the waist,

sunlight sprawled across an open window casing,
distant taxis, impatient running late for church,
and a nondescript bird somewhere nearby, calling,
fully expecting an answer.

Again

Like a closed door you've just enough room
to slip an envelope under—that's her smile.
Secretive, for a certain man, specific to her time,
which she leans away from toward us. Caught in her hair,
earrings that have been ornament to,
that have been lost and found by,
four families of women. Passed down, put on, taken off;
tossed on nightstands next to key sets and money clips;
maybe, now, beneath the seat of some junked car—
half-crushed, hauled cross country—half-hidden
in the granular silt of skin, baked dirt, and gravel dust,
an improbable glint
next to the pocket comb and the Viceroy wrapper.
That they have outlived the both of them,
that they were passed down at all is extraordinary enough.
Not pawned, not swapped with friends, not vacuumed up.
It has taken me thirty-seven years to understand
just how jewelry transcends its value,
that each piece in the museum has been worn,
has been breathed upon, coveted and caressed,
polished against a sleeve by some clandestine lover,
even if it was just the curator—
alone, bleary-eyed—dating, verifying.
They were banged up against door frames, snagged on cloth,
they met the enemy's face before the fist did,
they stood for something before the word did.
She had delicate wrists, the band says.
Such small hands, the ring says.
These earrings are shaped like wind chimes
and so announced every change in her,
as when the breeze picked up off the water
and opened the throat of her shirt
and the sun glanced off a collarbone for the first time.

Children have built whole worlds for them; men too.
And it doesn't matter whether copper or gold,
bones of small animals, or stones burnished smooth
by the flow of one small stream—the betrothals, the
bequeathings, all our precious extensions of the body.
Being seen, that's all we ask of this life—
to be acknowledged, to make
of what's been given us, each other,
and in the admiring, make something more,
again.

Linda's House of Beauty

is on the left, twelve minutes south of the black and white
cows, and two passing zones shy of where the bicycle man
will rest before the hill. In one hand he will hold his milk
gallon of water. In the other, the orange hunter's cap I just
saw on the ground. Here, I know where I am—the place I
am one song short of. Tuesday,

I was looking at the ground and when I pulled against
the door a woman was pushing it from the other side.
That surprised me and there was an odd feeling in my face
all the way to the cows. As if I wanted to smile
and drink at the same time, the way that cows seem
to want to say something while they chew.
That day, my fourteen-year-old saliva, the water that broke

the moment I was ready to be born, rearranged itself
in an astonishing sky. And I was guessing
she'd just come from Linda's.
She held a bottle of wine in both hands against
the new curve of her belly. There were thin lines
of snow along the stone fences
of the fields behind us.

I could be doing other things. I could drive a school bus
or make donuts. Or read gauges at the North Pole
for everybody. I could pedal slowly past the cows
and sing out to them like the old bicycle man.

Because I think that woman loved me for that moment.
I think the candles she must have lit that night
smelled like knee-high, unmown grass,

and when her husband messed her hair up she understood
I loved her back.

The Pier

Like a scarecrow pulled into halves
and shaken out for storage,
my shirt and jeans were drying above the tub.
I'd been in and out
of the bathroom all night, flustered
by childproof caps and tepid, chlorinated water,
and each time the clothes twisted toward me
on their hangers.

Maybe they were still dancing,
maybe they missed their closet at home,
maybe shirts and pants can miss each other,
feel useless on their own.
But like the sand ringing the corroded drain,
in exile from the hotel beach,
there was no sense to any pretense
we'd ever find a way back.

That day, I'd watched an elderly wife trail her husband
down to the sea, where he waited and they entered
at exactly the same time, then held to each other,
their waists disappearing and emerging in the waves.

They were like this for a good while, and I imagined
her calling him "baby" and him saying something silly,
like, "I'm glad I'm not a buoy without a gull,"
after which, she patted him on the swimsuit—
an almost imperceptible, fluid gesture beneath the water—
then moved toward the beach, as he, as if prompted by her,
began to swim to where the channel markers dip and bob,
pausing now and then to backstroke, so that he could
look at her looking for shells.

"No way, Jose,"
is what she said when he called to her.

I had dreamed all night of a man trying to teach me
his precisely convoluted way of tying trout flies.
It took me hours to get it, and then,
not only could I not pick up
the micro-thin leader to attach it,
but there was no water in the dream,
it was useless.

Waking then, it scared me, just how much
I wanted to be alone.

This was when I recalled the old bathers. And how
a young boy's kite shuddered and dove over our heads,
making a metallic, tearing sound in the wind,
like the zipper of a garment bag
big enough for all of us.
And how people sidled in thin strings along the pier,
whose pilings proceeded two by two out to sea.

Poem for the Name Mary

Like smoke in a bottle, like
hunger, sometimes light fits,
wraps itself around a person
or thing and doesn't let go.
The light becomes a name,
and that name becomes a voice
through which light speaks to us.
Maybe this is what a friend means
when she says there is a pair of lips
in the air, maybe this is desire
and need too. Or maybe
this is just how to love a potato,
how to see as the potato sees:
the childish, white arms that reach out
through its eyes into the dark of our cabinets
to bless them.

Grain

(after Vallejo and Justice)

I may die in Kansas on a cloudless day—
one of those wholesome weekends
between wheat conventions and gun shows
glazed over with plenty—
I may simply buckle
beneath the gold-flecked eyes of a carhop,
grasp at the little window tray
and never rise again.
The living blue of the sky
will no longer glance off my body,
my lips assume the tinge of Welch's grape juice,
my food grow cold.
These will bear witness to me:
twenty distracted tee-ball players
in three different makes of minivan.
Mark Cox will be dying. I will want
to utter "ambulance" as a last word on earth,
but it will sound like "ambitions."
I will want to say "my heart"
but it will be mistaken for "my art."
I will not want to leave you, love.
Our son, even if grown,
will be inching up the stair rail—
shin-deep in my work boots,
he will be going up
while I am going down—
and like a snapping turtle in a $2.00 butterfly net,
I will refuse the new world.
I will not want to leave my shirts emptied
over the backs of chairs,
I will not want to leave my toothbrush
leaning dry against yours,
I will have to be taken from you, love,

carried off by strong men
whose fathers sowed the grain fields around me,
it will take three of them, love,
I will remain so heavy with need for you,
so stubbornly loyal,
and even though I will be no more
than a quickly scrawled number next to the phone,
no more than a last breath not fully exhaled,
I will root myself in this earth of ours.
I will not rise through the air
nor dissolve into ground water,
I will not yearn for release
nor turn my face to the sky.
I will have to be taken on my side, love,
the way we lay together
when I was alive.

On the Way to See You

Pleasing. That simple
a word. Like a child and his dog drinking

from the same hose, one horse nuzzling another,
two birds sitting so close they seem
to have only two wings.

It's because I'm going to see you
I see these things.

Yesterday, I thought that dusk
was a kind of rain. Darkness fell and kept falling
until I believed it was something solid.

Now I see that when the blind remove their dark glasses,
when they put them on the bed stand before sleep,
there is a difference that they know.

This is when you smile the mysterious halfsmile
of those in love. Like miles of stone fence
on a moonlit pillow.

All of this because my eyes are already looking for you.
Because of you I can put my arm out the window

without fear. Because of you no tears
well in the spoons of these houses,
no one flinches

and the bodies of husbands and wives
are like warm bread to each other.

They believe that the moon

will touch the earth lightly on its waist
and the earth will turn.

I'm really going to see you, I know
because I really believe these things.
And because I believe them,

the cat slouching under that small tree
where the two wrens sat was driven away,
was beaten.

I know this now.
My skin feels pleasant suddenly
as the darkness veers around it.

And the dog sleeps lightly at the child's door.
And night is falling short of the ground.

Remarriage

He didn't have to taste them to know
they were bitter. Stunted, calcified,
clustered there, pale yellow and green,
the grapes seemed outgrowths
of the weathered trellis. The vines, of course,
always bore that tortured, arthritic posture,
but the fruits, these weren't to have happened
this way.

When she boiled them down, not even measuring
the sugar's cascade from the upended bag,
he thought, *I refuse to eat this
just to be nice.* He remembered the story
of his mother, how on the eve of her wedding
she ate three full meals so as not to insult her
two best friends. Perhaps it has become his story,
just having learned to say no. Perhaps it is
his father's story, he seems to wince
whenever it is told. His mother looks wan, nauseated.

Later, after the boiled jars had been cooled and filled,
after the paraffin had congealed, that first morning
while the bagels were browning, he sat across from her
as she tried to unscrew one lid. She made a
small moan, almost inaudible, then stopped,
tentatively handing it to him. And then,
after that moment of shame
in which he thought he couldn't open it,
he wiped his hand on a pants leg and turned
until it gave.

Patina

In my prime, shape presented first,
the contour and curve of one thing,
the sheer size of something else,
or the way her hair flowed volcanically

along each subtle slope and swell.
It was crazed, intense, super-heated,
even the soles of my boots felt sticky,

because she'd entered me, I knew this,
she was the ancient map of my blood,
and that twitch I sometimes suffered,
they blamed on stress and dehydration,

but it was her, pal, all her, she charted waters
I'd never named in myself,
she proffered the esprit, the joie de vivre, the élan,
that jackhammer of lust
beside the Fiesta Ware Outlet...

But one day, it just happens,
a man's eyes cloud and change,
you don't feel with the same ardor
the way she moves, her confident posture,

no, suddenly it is color you acknowledge,
the grays, the yellows, the bruised surfaces
tinged with a silver-green, almost a tarnish,
as if our skin were a metal,

and not such a precious one, either,
more like pewter or the common alloys
of soot-smudged medieval artisans,

something to be re-shaped, hammered thin,
become useful and used.

Quite all of a sudden,
your words are cast
with the hues of finality,
of last-ness and leave-taking.

What once called for passionate pyrotechnics,
requires, now, quietude and simplicity;
the clever words, the transatlantic words,
you have waved bon voyage to them,
their steamer trunks filled with dry husks,

while you, you're drifting the other way,
your hair silvering against the silver waters,
carried now by some lesser craft of language,
something more like a dimpled camp canoe,

toward some more nostalgic harbor
you vaguely remember having once named,
perhaps after a woman once loved, fiercely desired,
who was that now, who was that
and just what was it you really wanted?

7. Finish This

Rest Darling Sister Rest

The commas are the first to go,
well before periods, those
deeply drill-pressed holes denoting
what we know as last.
The dead don't need punctuation,
blended as they are
in equilibrium beyond syntax,
their final wishes and scripture
thinning on the thinning stone.

Solon's tuberculosis, Elizabeth's grief
at having outlived four fated children,
relieved now by the laying on of weather's hands.
For the body, it is as when the wedges of split wood
have burned long and deeply, softening enough
to collapse in halves and thirds onto the grate.
But the burning of stones is interminable and even,
the sun, day by day, fading the vinyl
of mobile homes beside the graveyard,
oblong mausoleums lit nightly
with the blue wash of TV.

Sometimes I stop at the spigots,
fill the watering can caretakers provide,
and douse the driest, neglected flowers—
sometimes I just drive past.
Or sometimes, my car's aerodynamics
a bit too coffin-like,
I just walk from grave to grave,
sensing the give of the earth,
the vaults' contours, the water lines'
criss-cross grid above the bones.

If there's anything left to be said,
I don't know what it is.
I just repeat what the stones say.
And the wind, as you've guessed already,
will have the last word, anyway.

The Chain

The neighbors had their lawn plowed
and now chunks of sod punctuate
a sloped bank of snow
that will be weeks thawing. They did so
to accommodate the mourners, whose cars,
ticking as they steamed and cooled,
have congregated all afternoon,
their owners trickling in and out,
feet stuttering on the icy parts,
casseroles held to one side
so as to better watch each step.

And the house, the house itself
is nearly animate with sorrow—
icicles snap free of eaves,
piercing the snow, irregular slabs of snow
slide whole from the metal roof,
smoke unspools from the chimney, wrenched
from the wood-stove in a diagonal so taut
one's stomach hurts.

But inside, I know, there is a stillness,
a layer of it, like the ice
a river runs beneath,
and the people slipping there,
grasping at words,
can feel the hair on their bodies
rubbing against their clothes, distrust
the way silverware darkens
when they move their arms.

It's this calm that *is* the storm:
the middle of you

dropping to its knees, right there inside you,
in front of everybody, though outwardly,
no sign of change but the trousers pooling
at the tops of your shoes;
the stiff, leather-bound guest book
of another's life closing itself,
page over page,
alone on the desk at the other side
of the room.

At their back door, I rub his old dog's head.
Her wet fur moves freely over her skull,
and for the first time there is a skipping
in her breath, as if she's losing traction.
Yet, I've never seen her seem happier,
or less inclined to push her way inside.
She has the cars, this snow, the crackers
some small boy has tossed just beyond
her length of chain. And this is more
than enough, being all she knows.

Finish This

When gram died, her last act
was to hand back a Dixie cup
half trembling with water
as if to say, "Here, finish this."
My mother took it, separating the fingers,
thin and glossy with illness,
then guiding the whole arm down
to its place across her chest.
I was on the other side,
the hospital bed rail
pushing one cool shirt button into me
as if I were a doorbell. "I'm out here,"
Death was saying, "We don't have a lot of time,
you coming or not?"
The railing gave a little, sideways,
and since there was nothing left
but those most accidental of sounds—
the involuntary frictions of left/right,
up/down, in/out,
the sound of a loose tire iron
in the back of my pickup,
of two swords
meeting farther and farther away—
that final letting go of the guard
by which all week she had pulled herself up toward me,
was a release into silence, a recognition
of the true completeness of every gesture.
And having relayed to me that dry, barely tangible kiss,
she could stop now, thereby seeming calmly to recede.
Outside, the cold white ashes of eons
piled high against the curbs
and Death leaned on his shovel
near a narrow, salted path into underground parking,

and the truck stalled,
and it seemed for a moment,
the past so completely with me, so heavy and sodden,
I'd never turn the key again.
That was when I remembered the little Dixie cup,
the pale purple lilacs ringing its lip,
and how my mother raised it like a shot glass to her own mouth
then chose merely to sip.

White Tornado

In commercials it spirals from room to room:
breadcrumbs, bacon grease, fingerprints
get erased and you don't have to do anything.
Just unscrew the cap and get out of the way.
When it's over, even the lady's dress is clean,
her hair has been done, and sunlight streams
all at once into the kitchen like a happy child
with flowers.

Like hell, he thinks. Everybody knows
that memory is just a vacuum cleaner
with a filter we can't replace—
it spews out as much as it can take in, clarify,
so you work hard forever
in a haze you just get used to.

Most dust is human skin—sprinkles
on the vanilla cone of survivorship, sustenance
for the little fish who can't cut it on the bottom.
You do what you know—burning your fingers
on thin Styrofoam cups, parting your mouth
against the small bowl of a shaving mirror—
while they roll to one side
and float helplessly up through you
toward the silken scoop of forgiveness
on its wire handle.

After the *Today Show* he will proceed to the medicine cabinet.
He will wave like a mother at a summer camp bus,
its mirror will be free of the lint of her...
But it's hard having nothing to lean against but the sink.
And though there'll be nothing he can't see then,
he'll be all that is.

Pulsar

There is an unsettling dailiness
to letters of the dead—
they shook the rain from their umbrellas,
they dried their socks on radiators—
but like a gnat balanced
on the hair of their arms,
the pressure of death was always there,

and he who is left to read
now bears it also,
a constant usually assimilated
like the hum of the fluorescent light
he reads by,
becomes, now, irrevocable silence,
a door opening
onto the particular frictions of things:
wind streaming between eave vents,
rain thipping at glass,
his own blood just beneath the skin.

He, left living, opens his eyes
on another day he can't keep from happening,
every window an open wound
smeared with sunlight
the yellow of grass beneath a patio block,
birds bickering in the pom-poms
of trees that top his building,
and beyond, embedded light years
in the unfathomed reaches of the psyche,
the cold, dead planets of his wife and children,
the meteorites of friends and family,
all the broken techno-junk and orbiting debris,
circle their dying star—

he, who cannot move to lift his brush to his teeth,
yet who shudders with the energy he has no choice
but to have.

The Salvation Army has been by
for its black garbage bags of clothing—
in thrift shops, city-wide,
the belt buckles, the bracelets, the Tonka trucks
and reading glasses—all the shaped minerals and metals,
the leathers, the woods, have been racked and tagged,
are to be dispersed,

to live out their time, like light in space,
as mere projections of their origins—
their courses fixed, though severed utterly,
their presence felt, though indiscernible—
irreducible, yet gone.

Kodachrome

We don't show these family slides much,
in part, because the projector overheats,
but also because we miss my father's litanies
of the dead and their diseases:
congestive heart failure; cirrhosis; even gangrene—
their ravaged, cancer-eaten, over-stressed organs
recalled in official diagnoses,
each dry account closing
while the next was ratcheted into place,
dad pressing the wired remote
as if it were the release button on a bombsight.

To counterbalance, we kids attend less
to people than to things: the Coleman cooler
intact after thirty-seven years;
the spangled (barely) red felt stockings
in which we still stuff memory cards and batteries;
the untouched Hai Karate cologne; the flight jacket
Mom's threatened for fifty-five years to toss.
It's funny, self-deprecatory, even vaguely reassuring
until we get to the chilling reverse family portrait
in which we sat on the same couch
we're now watching from,
looking forward to ourselves, some new upholstery,
and a smaller dog at our feet. There's just
enough time for a last inside joke, for recognizing
the hard candy in its dish, pretending to spit out
the piece now diminishing in my mouth,
before the tone is torqued flush with our mortality.

Those endless summers weren't. Without Dad,
we can barely manage to find the same room,
let alone the Black Hills or Mount Rushmore.

There are people in these slides even Mother
can't remember, overtaken, as she is
by the ghosts of her dead.
Yet we press onward into one last box,
burdened now by our own youthful faces
and the betrayal of those bodies,
vigorous and unblemished as they are,
there in the silence of celluloid,
ready for anything, except, that is, this.

Black Olives

Cooking was, at first, a problem not worth solving;
he wasn't really hungry and it took days
to eat the leftovers. But after the funeral,
while opening a can of soup, he understood
that despite fifty years of meals,
there was not one morsel left.

There were no doubt some several million diners
to whom this did not matter much in October of 1977,
but in the grayed light of her kitchen,
at the faux marble-topped table for two,
my grandfather added and multiplied and estimated,
and when he was done,
proposed to have an accurate accounting
of how many tons grandmother had cooked.
It was something he had to know.
And he could not be bothered to eat until he did.

And even this was not enough, no, he had to illustrate,
he had to concretize, he had to guess how many silos
her labor would have emptied. How many acres
were planted, how many loaves were baked, how many
animals, by type, had marched two by two into our mouths.

When he finished it was dusk and his soup was cold.
He let us have a pizza delivered—mushroom and black olives—
and we laughed, a little weakly, at just how much gram would
have hated what he'd done. How she always glazed over
when he computed mileage per gallon. But she had loved
black olives—those tiny bitter, hollowed hearts—
she'd eaten how many, let's see, how many would that be...?

Pissing Off Robert Frost's Porch

For Bill Matthews

Not the side of a rowboat, granted—
no rising and falling on the wash of tides.
One drink, in honor of you, now dispersed
over daylilies and lupine as the sky Frost knew
resists its darkening, turns slate,
then charcoal gray, an operatic note
held longer than light can hope for.
What we take in, clarify, is temporary;
we pass through each other, heard again
and filtered through the views
to which we're predisposed.
No ocean here, so far from home.
That death's-head moth, I know,
is neither him nor you.
The one dim candle that draws it forth
belongs, however briefly, to simple me.
And now the dogs express concern,
four or five along the valley's mile.
It will be dark until the earth has turned.
It will be dark now, for a while.

Thespian

To have delivered his deathbed part,
to have exposed for all of us,
the final seams of lips and eyelids;
to have withheld on the ten-count our own
panic for breath, then, emptied
of the desperate operatic note —
the stilled pose,
the shared curtain's close,
the shovelful of applause on his coffin lid —
to have arisen from that grave.

What a gift, to cleanse the grease paint from one's face,
to feel one's arms suspending, to feel
the faint strings detach from elbow, wrist and fingers,
to rise again from the lit mirror, to part your robe,
then, to stand in privacy, urinating, thirsty.

In This His Suit

Not his clothes, but their chimerical creases.
Not his body, but the gestures of his body
worn last and put unpressed
into its plastic. Not the hand,
but how he held it, palm buttressing head.
Not the meat, not words, but grace; not the mouth,
but the smoke, scratches on a plate,
the table's dulled edge.
Not absence, not presence. Not indentation,
but impression. Not not, but not is; not either
or neither. The hose's curve, the garden's
mounds, the slab walk's slope, the smell of the smell,
the sound of the sound, the book's missing page
found in another book.
Not the death, but his dying.
Not male, not female, not young, old, compassionate,
bitter, peaceful or sorrowed.
Not the life, but the living.

Things My Grandfather Must Have Said

I want to die in the wintertime,
make the ground regret it,
make the backhoe sweat.

January. Blue Monday
after the holiday weekend.
I want it to be hard on everybody.

I want everyone to have a headache
and the traffic to be impossible.
Back it up for miles, Jesus.

I want steam under the hood, bad directions,
cousins lost, babies crying, and sleet.
I want a wind so heavy their umbrellas howl.

And give me some birds, pigeons even,
anything circling for at least half an hour,
and plastic tulips and a preacher who stutters

"Uh" before every word of Psalm 22.
I want to remind them just how bad things are.
Spell my name wrong on the stone, give me

earthworms fat as Aunt Edith's arms
surfacing under the folding chairs.
And I want a glass coffin,

I want to be wearing the State of Missouri
string tie that no one else liked....God,
I hope the straps break

and I fall in with a thud. I hope

the shovel slips out of my son's hands.
I want them to remember I don't feel anything.

I want the food served straight from my garden.
I want the head of the table set. I want
everyone to get a pennant that says,

"Gramps was the greatest,"
and a complete record of my mortgage payments
in every thank-you note.

And I want to keep receiving mail for thirteen years,
all the bills addressed to me,
old friends calling every other month

to wonder how I am.
Then I want an earthquake or rising water-table,
the painful exhumation of my remains.

I want to do it all again.

I want to die the day before something truly
important happens and have my grandson ask:
What would he have thought of that?

I want you all to know how much I loved you.

8. After Rain

Sonata

At ninety, the piano plays him.
He's like a man by the sea
the wind knows it must wear down,
sculpt to a profile,
then fill out again,
billowing his sleeves and trouser legs
into a younger musculature.
Over and again, the music grays
then reddens, the part
in its hair shifting left to center
until those few blades of sea grass
are all that's left to be
combed over the rocks,
and the thin fingers skitter,
leaving impressions in the keyboard
that waves wash level,
cleansing its audience of shell halves,
now glistening, now scoured dry.
And the house, the house just outside
this sonata's frame,
begs him to turn around
to pick his way back
along the stony runner,
his hands stopping his ears.
But, at ninety, the music plays the piano,
which plays the man, who finally, fearlessly,
plays himself, which is the landscape,
which is everything that ends.

Eastern Wyoming

Why hide where we can see you?
Because you could not find me

Why turn from fires to the outer dark?
Because the moth among sparks becomes a spark

How long can a flower be held and still be a flower?
There is no end to the ground of your hand

If the hand opens, where will the fist fall?
The fist is always a fist and grows again on your arm

How can the tree in granite flourish?
*Because its root is memory. And because one
brakeman stopped to give it water*

How can we go on this way?
There is not enough room in the world to turn your life around

Poem at 40

Wind-washed—as if standing next to the highway,
a truck long as the century sweeping by,
all things at last bent in the same direction.
An opening, as if all
the clothes my ancestors ever wore
dry on lines in my body—
windwhipped, parallel with the ground,
some sleeves sharing a single clothespin
so that they seem to clasp hands,
seem to hold on.

And now that I can see
up the old women's dresses,
there's nothing but a filtered light.
And now that their men's smoky breath
has traversed the earth,
it has nothing to do with them.
And now that awkward, fat tears of rain
slap the window screen,
now that I'm naked too,
cupping my genitals, tracing with a pencil
the blue vein between my collar bone and breast,
I'll go to sleep when I'm told.

At the Stair

Adulthood's frost heaves tamped down,
that blank page smoothed,

a last glance up,
palm on the burnished rail.

That night, so many nights ago,
that house still as this one is now,

and you, sleepless below the attic dormer,
your face cold, quilts heavy as soil,

all the wind-burnt children, hearts quieted,
your snow tunnels welling with moonlight,

the farmyard evanescent
with mist and thickening ice.

How many splitting, warping, hand-hewn steps
between there and here, no elders

left at Scrabble around the kitchen table?
Unpoured and prepared again to be,

is this too much to ask?
To come to that young body

as to the mouth of a cave,
to reenter it and find

one's final shape in the accruing snow?

Heart on Stilts

Once accepted, the interludes of silence and wind
become a kind of harmonic frequency
middle age can finally hear; recurrences
that belie the chaos of each roiling inlet.
And so, within the hoarse warnings

of tugs and open water buoys,
the tide arrives as if called to supper,
rising indiscernibly up pilings, stretching taut
the chains of channel markers, flooding, once again,
the marshlands' primordial ruin.

Any husband wading here in this cove of bent grasses
and cell towers, knows that within the shifting breeze
of youth he can only skitter among shorebirds,
head down, solitary, mindful of dark currents,
the sustaining sea's ancient threat.

Better there, on the suspended pier of love and grace,
inept as he may be. A grown man
no longer longs to lay himself down
with the gray and supple sea,
to be held in its blank arms, but rather

for inducements to make a way home,
subsumed by traffic along the guy-wired palmettos,
his beach towel held like a child to his chest,
toward all that need him
and thus all he really needs.

Natural Causes

Because my son saw the round hay bales—
1200 pounds apiece, shrink-wrapped in white plastic—
lining the fields,
we have had to search all evening
for marshmallows.
Two stores were out. Another
had one stale and shrunken bag.
The fourth had three bags, but no wood for fire,
so we went back to the first.
And I needed newspaper to start the kindling,
which is how I know Earl Softy died Monday,
at home, in his sleep, of natural causes. So rarely
we know how we know what we know.
Don't turn the page. Sit with us awhile,
here by the fire in New Hampshire.
Have a marshmallow.
Because my wife and I love each other
and wanted something of, and more than, ourselves;
because my little son has imagined heaven in the pasture land,
even death tastes sweet.

Duende

The music played at your oldest friend's wake —
the last who knew the first girl you kissed

who knew you pissed the bed still at twelve
and how you shook shamed with fear
but rode the wild horse and did not fall —

the song aired as he lies in his casket
unable to know again
ever forever

is so beautiful
you can't decide
whether to cry out or sing

Ashes, Ashes

Snow. A nit's weight
on the hair of one's neck,
the blessed host of the past,
right there, just so.
Turn into it, this once.
It's time to become the lake surface,
time to claim your face.

Soon the present
will cool enough to touch,
you can lay you down
in the outline you once were,

smoke still adrift
from the original fire.
Cup the moth's spark
in your hands.
Open your mouth and take
the dissolution
on your tongue.

No one else remembers
exactly what you remember.
If you don't carry it,
who will?

The Will

I am about to — or, I am going to —
die: either expression is correct.

— Dominique Bouhours
French grammarian, d. 1702)

Tilting my head, watching car lights wind
down the mountain, I realize
how easily the mountain moves.
It's in flames on the glass of our window,
like our faces in those flames,
while the one cloud, backlit, and pausing
briefly along the top of the mountain,
rains out there beyond us,
yet inside us too.

What we have is here to be seen through.
Cinnamon tea welling in our spoons,
steam rising
off the dog still trembling near the hearth —
we've made plans.

I sought for a town among mountains, once;
a little Greek town where the wind
would put its soft mouth to the houses
in the one chord I could sleep to.
When the windows chattered restless in casings there
it would feel good to shiver in the dark with them.
And upon closing my eyes I would see through the earth
and fall to a space where time ruled so gently
that the stars could cease their blinking. A car
turning the corner could lay its white hand on my forehead,
but I'd know it was God.

" 'Light! More light!' " you ask,

"Whose last words were those?"
Then, " 'Put out that bloody cigarette…' "
which were H. H. Munro's. How easily
that German bullet translated his individuated voice,
even as he attempted to stay entrenched in the dark.

Today, when the dog dropped your stick
at my feet, and shook the lake from himself
I was shocked by the cold he'd just as soon return to.
But when I looked at the water, it was a Greek woman

standing and smoothing her dress, and I knew
that wherever we're going it won't be cold at all,
it won't be permanent. The wavering, the flickering,
the motion is what matters.

After Rain

Sometimes, night quieted,
what's real soaks in further;
the mesh screens gemmed by halogen,
my neighbors' doorbell switch
like a moon within reach,
the lilies nodding on their stems
like exhausted horsemen.
Denied the old illusion of ownership,
I have opened somehow,
but for once, nothing is leaving or lessened.

The journey is long.
The journey is not long.
Moths drink their fill at the screens,
the caught rain glistening.
What conscious moment
is not, in essence, worship;
what state more vulnerable
than the attentive mind upturned?

We bear forth our sparks, from psychic fire,
each family a series of contained blazes,
each patio torch a signal pyre,
our longing eternal,
and though the skin thins,
our inner lives grow cold,
there is always, this black frock
nightfall offers—
the comfort, finally,
of tenderness and humility and weakness,
the calm after rain
and before the slate's clearing.

After Reading Tu Fu,

I compose myself. I button my shirt,
align my script as precisely as I can.
To be in the presence of great absence
requires a posture of respect.

The candle of day still feeds on his breath.
The one massing cloud, variously shaded,
draws his shroud across the mountain's face.
Once I am finished, I will follow.

Though who can say where finished is.

Acknowledgments

The author wishes to thank the editors of the following magazines, in which new poems appeared or were reprinted:

The Café Review: "Palm Springs"

Inlandia: A Literary Journey: "Palm Springs"

The Lightning Key Review: "Being Here"

New California Writing 2013: "Palm Springs"

New Ohio Review: "All That Shimmers and Settles Along the Roads of Our Passage," "The Briefcase," "Dunes," "Patina," "Alcohol," and "Kodachrome."

Poetry: "Lemon Icing"

The Ink Quill: "Cassandra by a Nose," "Morality Play"

The Raleigh News-Observer: "Heart on Stilts"

"Meridian" was completed for, and first appeared in, *The Heart's Many Doors: American Poets Respond to Metka Krašovec's Images Responding to Emily Dickinson*, Wings Press, edited by Richard Jackson.

"After Rain," "After Reading Tu Fu," "At the Crematorium, My Son Asks Why We're All Wearing Black," "At the Stair," "Ashes, Ashes," "Better Homes and Gardens," "Dark Black," "Eastern Wyoming," "Fatherhood," "Finish This," "Inner Rooms," "Joyland," "Natural Causes," "On the Way to See You," "Pail of Eggs," "Pissing Off Robert Frost's Porch," Pompeii," "Red Lead, 1978," "Rest Darling Sister Rest," "Sill," "Treasure," and "Want" from *Natural Causes: Poems,* by Mark Cox, © 2004. Reprinted by permission of the University of Pittsburgh Press.

"Again," "Black Olives," "The Chain," "The Chair of Forget-fulness," "Compass," "The Door," "Get Me Again," "Grain," "Like A Simile," "Make the Cobra Talk," "The Moles," "Party of One," "The Pier," "Poem at 40," "Pulsar," "Remarriage," "The River," "Sonata," "Still Life with Motion," "A Stone," and "The Tunnel at the End of the Light" from *Thirty-Seven Years from the Stone,* by Mark Cox, © 1998. Reprinted by permission of the University of Pittsburgh Press

"The Angelfish," "The Barbells of the Gods," "Divorce," "Don-ald," "Fugitive Love," "Geese," "In This His Suit," "Linda's House of Beauty," "The Pale and Hairless Ankles of the Sun," "Poem for the Name Mary," "The Will," "Rubbing Dirt from My Dog's Nose, I Realize...," "Running My Fingers Through My Beard on Bolton Road," "Simile at the Side of the Road," "Sorrow Bread," "Things My Grandfather Must Have Said," "Where," "White Tornado," "Why is That Pencil Always Behind Your Ear?," "The Word" first appeared in *Smoulder,* David R. Godine, Publisher, by Mark Cox, ©1989 and are reprinted here by right of the author.

I want to thank friends for their support of this work over the years: Ralph Angel, Nancy Card, Stuart Dischell, Mark Doty, Keith Earnshaw, Philip Gerard, Tony Hoagland, Cynthia Hun-tington, Richard Jackson, David Jauss, Bret Lott, David Rivard, Jill Rosser, Mary Ruefle, Betsy Sholl, Jean-Anne Sutherland, Leslie Ullman, Gordon Weaver, Roger Weingarten and David Wojahn. I also want to thank my editor and publisher, Walter Cummins, for going far beyond the call of duty with the manu-script and for taking such care with this book.

I am grateful to the University of North Carolina Wilmington for a research reassignment when some of this work was completed.

Notes and Dedications:

p. 93 and p. 96 "Make the Cobra Talk" and "Get Me Again" are for my son, Austin Hartsook.

p. 103 and p. 111 "Want" and "Fatherhood" are for my son, Keith.

p. 91 and p.104 "Sill" and "To My Daughter, Turning 16" are for my daughter, Rachel.

p. 141 "Pissing Off Robert Frost's Porch" is for Bill Matthews.

p. 27 "The Tunnel at the End of the Light" is for David Rivard, who titled it.

p. 78 "The Chair of Forgetfulness" is for Karin Gottshall and Tony Hoagland.

p. 120 "Grain" is for my former wife, Karin.

p. 4 "The Word" partially owes its origins to Stephen Berg's "On This Side of The River."

p. 82 In "Fugitive Love," the line: "the tearing and merging of clouds" is the title of a poem by Russell Edson.

p. 74 "Divorce" is for Ben Mitchell.

p. 76 "Joyland" is for Bret Lott.

p. 8 "All That Shimmers and Settles Along the Roads of Our Passage" is for my former wife, Rita Kilpatrick.

p. 58 "Emergen(ce) of Feeling" is for Emily Carr.

p. 119 "Poem for the Name Mary" is for Mary La Chapelle.

About the Author

MARK COX has previously published four volumes of poetry: *Barbells of the Gods* (Ampersand Press), *Smoulder* (David R. Godine), *Thirty-Seven Years from the Stone*, and *Natural Causes* (both in the Pitt Poetry Series). *Readiness*, a new book of prose poems is slated for publication in 2018. Cox has a 30-year publication history in prominent magazines and has received a Whiting Writers Award, a Pushcart Prize, and numerous fellowships for that work. He teaches in the Department of Creative Writing at University of North Carolina Wilmington and in the Vermont College MFA Program.

Made in the USA
San Bernardino, CA
25 May 2017